Who was Dr Jackson?

Dr John Jackson

Who was Dr Jackson?
Two Calcutta Families: 1830 - 1855

by

Mary Bennett

BACSA

PUTNEY, LONDON
2002

Published by the British Association
for Cemeteries in South Asia (BACSA)

Secretary: Theon Wilkinson MBE
76½ Chartfield Avenue
London SW15 6HQ

The British Association for Cemeteries in South Asia was formed in 1976 to
preserve, convert and record old European cemeteries. All proceeds from the
sale of this book go towards this charity. (Registered No 273422)

ISBN 0 907799 78 7

British Libraries Cataloguing-in-Publication Data
A catalogue record for this book is available from the British Library

Map and plan adapted by Rosemarie Wilkinson

Typeset by Professional Presentation, 3 Prairie Road, Addlestone, Surrey

Printed by The Chameleon Press Ltd., 5-25 Burr Road, Wandsworth SW18 4SG

Contents

Illustrations

*   *   *

Small lithographic sketches by Colesworthy Grant at breaks in text:
*Country Hospital Ward, Palkee-carriage, Hooghli-boat,
The Flying Dak, Dak Bungalow, River steamer*

*   *   *

Notes on Colesworthy Grant

The lithographs reproduced in the book are taken from the following books by Colesworthy Grant, published in Calcutta:

Lithographic Sketches of the Public Characters of Calcutta, published in various local technical and sporting journals, 1838 to 1850. *(Courtesy of the Oriental & India Office Collections of the British Library)*

Anglo-Indian Domestic Life, published anonymously in 1862

Rural Life in Bengal; Illustrative of Anglo-Indian Suburban Life, anon. 1860

Colesworthy Grant was born in London in 1813 and sailed to Calcutta in 1832 to take up a post as Drawing master at the Howrah Engineering College, becoming Professor of Drawing in the 1850s. Among other works referred to above, he illustrated Dr Mouat's *Atlas of Anatomy*. He died in Calcutta in 1880.

Foreword

Who was Dr Jackson? is the thirty-second in our series of books about Europeans in South Asia, written by BACSA members, published by BACSA with a wider public in mind. It should appeal particularly to those interested in following a distinguished medical career in India against a fascinating family background which included the Corries, Pattles, Prinseps and Camerons, all in positions of influence during the good doctor's twenty-five unbroken years service in India with its enforced separation from his wife and daughters.

The book is based on letters from the doctor to his wife and eldest daughter in London which reflect the loneliness of the separation he endured when pen and ink provided the only link with his three girls growing-up in an entirely different literary environment in London. The book also draws on the journal of his aunt who lived with him in Calcutta for many years and provided some lively side-lights on Calcutta society. By some serendipity which seems to attach to these ancestral memoirs, the portrait print of the aunt was seen to be by Colesworthy Grant which led to alighting by chance on his series of lithographic sketches published in various sporting and medical journals at the time, bringing vividly to life a number of the characters featured here. It is a fascinating study of two families with their Calcutta-Bloomsbury connections.

The author is a great-granddaughter of Doctor Jackson and is already known to BACSA readers through her biography of her maternal grandfather's family, the Ilberts which spans British-Indian affairs from a political angle.

Introduction and Acknowledgements

Dr Jackson, the maternal grandfather of Virginia Woolf, is one of those who have no memorial. Students of Bloomsbury brush him aside as of no interest. In this way they follow the line taken by his son-in-law, Leslie Stephen (Mrs Woolf's father), who dismissed 'the worthy doctor' as a dull, sensible man, remarkable only for iron health and a fine head of hair, considered a good physician in Calcutta, not up to his wife. But was this really all that he was? The question seemed worth asking if only on account of all the other grandchildren. The Jackson daughters married intelligent and capable men, but with the exception of Stephen they made less of their lives than might have been expected from their abilities. The next generation was notably successful. By the time I was growing up, in the early nineteen-thirties, five of the twelve grandsons were dead, killed by war, disease or the two together: the professional soldier, the architect, the lifelong invalid thought the cleverest of the lot by his siblings, and the two whose combination of vigorous mind and splendid looks made each seem rather larger than life to his contemporaries, Thoby Stephen, just starting at the Bar, and Charles Fisher, an Oxford don. There remained my father, HAL Fisher, a historian who had been President of the Board of Education in the Lloyd George administrations and was now Head of his Oxford College, his cousin and exact contemporary WW Vaughan, Headmaster of Rugby School, his surviving brothers, William, Commander-in-Chief Mediterranean Fleet and Commander-in-Chief Home Fleet, and Edwin, Chairman of Barclays Bank, the two Duckworth cousins, George, a successful public servant and Gerald, founder of the eponymous publishing house, and Adrian Stephen, a doctor and early disciple of Freud. I never knew the two last; but the five kindly, authoritative men whom I did know were far from negligible. Did they owe nothing to their grandfather? I thought in a rather desultory way that it would be interesting to find out.

The first stage was straightforward, if only because the work was done by others. Dr Richard Bingle equipped me with the official record of Dr Jackson's Indian service and drew my attention to what was to prove a key connection with the family of Archdeacon Daniel Corrie. The archivists of the Royal Colleges of Physicians and of Surgeons added more dates and facts and put up with a lot of ignorant enquiries. Mrs Suzanne Mendel of *Laurie Ancestry* in Lincolnshire rapidly provided the Doctor with parents and a background in Bengal as well as in Lincolnshire. The bones were there but there was not much flesh to put on them.

At this stage it was suggested to me that my cousin, John Vaughan, might possibly know of some family papers. He immediately produced the packet of letters that form the core of this book, Dr Jackson came to life. At the same time the focus shifted. Letters written by a father to a child on the other side of the world may not individually be of particular interest, but taken together these seemed to me to give a picture of family life divided between England and Calcutta in the second quarter of the nineteenth century that was worth preserving on its own account, irrespective of any light that it might throw on the character of the writer. The picture became all the sharper on the discovery of the diary of Dr Jackson's aunt, Mrs Ellerton, who lived in his house while his wife was in England, a peculiarly lively witness to the divide between the evangelical puritanism of his own connections and the very different ethos of his in-laws, the Pattles. This diary was tracked down on my behalf by Mr Christopher Walker of the Department of Western Antiquities in the British Museum, a direct descendant of its writer, who has also furnished the portrait of his formidable ancestress reproduced on page 35 and patiently answered my questions about his forbears. To him, as to John Vaughan, I owe a debt of deepest gratitude for allowing me a free run of these two interlocking sets of papers, both now deposited in the Oriental and India Office Collections of the British Library.

In putting the record together I have been saved from a number of bad mistakes by Mr John Beaumont, who generously allowed me to see in draft his substantial revision of the paper on *The Chevalier de l'Etang and his Descendants* written for private circulation by Sir Hugh Orange in the 1930s; a shortened version of this study has since been published in the *Virginia Woolf Bulletin* of 2001 and the full text deposited in the JM Cameron Archives at Freshwater on the Isle of Wight. I have asked for and received help from cousins of every degree and from friends in and out of Oxford and must particularly thank Olivier Bell, Julia Emsden, Ann Steadman, Vanessa Winchester and again John Vaughan for providing illustrations, Dr Tom Patterson and Dr Mark Harrison for bibliographical advice, and Dr Jane Mellanby for taking the trouble to read Dr Jackson's opusculum on tetanus. Staff in the London Library and in the Indian Institute Library in Oxford have been helpful as ever, and Mr David Blake in the Oriental and India Office Collections of the British Library particularly resourceful in digging out useful files. Theon Wilkinson and Richard Bingle have provided moral support throughout, to say nothing of occasional help with Dr Jackson's handwriting, and in the final stages when I was temporarily out of action have picked up dropped stitches and tied up loose ends that I ought to have dealt with myself. And Olivia Milburn has typed and retyped with unfailing patience, accuracy and speed.

In the end I have become very fond of Dr Jackson. I don't say that my spirits would soar if I were to find myself sitting next to him at dinner but I would gladly set out on a difficult journey in his company. He seems to me to have left his mark on a great many of his descendants, not only where it might be expected, as with my naval uncle William (surely in direct line from the mariner who kept his ship happy and orderly in the China Seas two hundred years ago?), but also where it is unexpected, as with Mrs Leslie Stephen. But it is idle to try to disentangle the hereditary plait. I leave 'the worthy doctor' to make his own case.

Oxford 2002   Mary Bennett

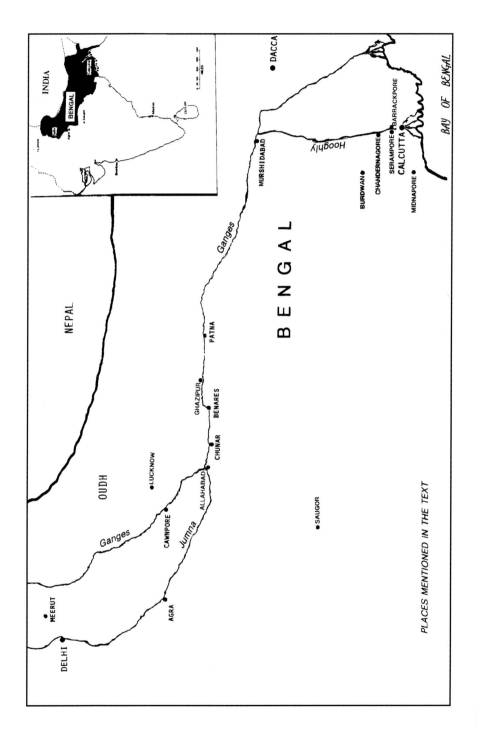

PLACES MENTIONED IN THE TEXT

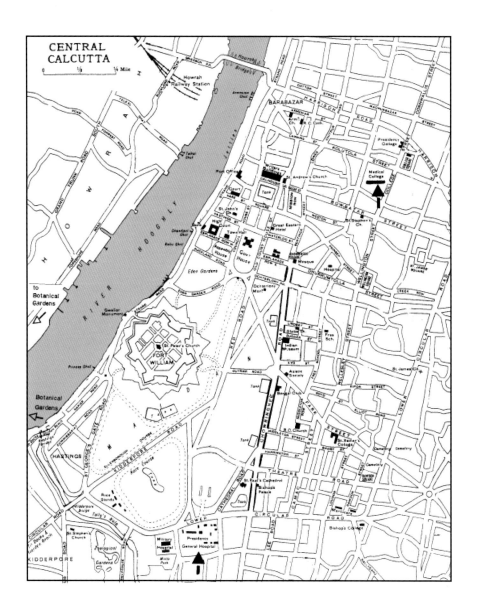

Family

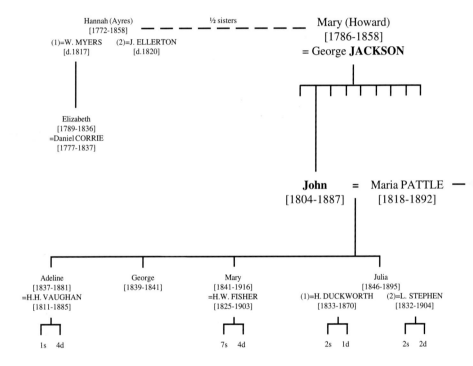

Hannah (Ayres)
[1772-1858]
(1)=W. MYERS   (2)=J. ELLERTON
[d.1817]   [d.1820]

— — — ½ sisters — — — —

Mary (Howard)
[1786-1858]
= George **JACKSON**

Elizabeth
[1789-1836]
=Daniel CORRIE
[1777-1837]

John = Maria PATTLE
[1804-1887] [1818-1892]

Adeline
[1837-1881]
=H.H. VAUGHAN
[1811-1885]

1s 4d

George
[1839-1841]

Mary
[1841-1916]
=H.W. FISHER
[1825-1903]

7s 4d

Julia
[1846-1895]
(1)=H. DUCKWORTH (2)=L. STEPHEN
[1833-1870]   [1832-1904]

2s 1d   2s 2d

Trees

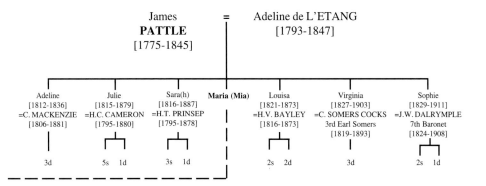

James **PATTLE** [1775-1845] = Adeline de L'ETANG [1793-1847]

Adeline	Julie	Sara(h)	**Maria (Mia)**	Louisa	Virginia	Sophie
[1812-1836]	[1815-1879]	[1816-1887]		[1821-1873]	[1827-1903]	[1829-1911]
=C. MACKENZIE	=H.C. CAMERON	=H.T. PRINSEP		=H.V. BAYLEY	=C. SOMERS COCKS	=J.W. DALRYMPLE
[1806-1881]	[1795-1880]	[1795-1878]		[1816-1873]	3rd Earl Somers	7th Baronet
					[1819-1893]	[1824-1908]
3d	5s 1d	3s 1d		2s 2d	3d	2s 1d

1
Jacksons and Pattles

I have always known what my great-grandfather Jackson looked like. He was the sturdy old gentleman with the halo of white hair and whiskers in the collection of family photographs that hung over the fireplace in my father's study. What he was like as a person was less evident. The outline was clear enough: he came from Lincolnshire; then he practised as a doctor in Bengal for twenty-five years without once coming home; he married one of the seven daughters of a senior Bengal civilian, James Pattle, and his beautiful French wife; he had three daughters of his own and twenty-three grandchildren, of whom the most remarkable was Virginia Woolf. The inscribed silver inkstand that my father always used added the information that certain 'native graduates of the Calcutta Medical College' had on some occasion wished to testify to his personal kindness and superior professional skill. That was about all. No legends clung to him, as they did in abundance to his wife's family. He apparently spoke very little about himself. What, if anything, was behind that rather splendid patriarchal appearance?

Not much, in the opinion of Virginia Woolf's father, his son-in-law Leslie Stephen. 'Not a man of any great mark... would as soon have visited his patients in his shirt-sleeves as resigned his Thirty-nine Articles.' (Stephen had himself moved comparatively painlessly from holy orders to vigorous agnosticism). 'A worshipper of respectability... in imperfect sympathy with the poetical and lofty aspect of things.'[1] A different side was seen by the poet Coventry Patmore, a longstanding friend of both Jacksons (and a rather sentimental witness), who wrote after his death that Dr Jackson had 'long attained that serene and thorough goodness which I have been all my life in vain endeavouring to reach... I have never seen him without being rebuked by such gentle

1

perfection.'[2] For my father, Herbert Fisher, one of the eldest of his grandchildren, he opened the door to the fascination of India. When an old friend from Indian days visited, 'we children, skirmishing round the fringes of a conversation of which we could understand only the merest fragments, were made to feel the presence of the mysterious East, with its peacocks and elephants, its temples and lakes, its veiled princesses and jewelled princes, and wondered why our grandparents had ever exchanged such splendours and delights for the quiet comforts of their Kentish home,'[3] he wrote. To my youngest Fisher aunt, Dr Jackson was simply 'that dear old man.'

These are all memories of a man whose active life was in the past. In the letters that follow in the second part of this book, written from India when he was in his forties, Dr Jackson speaks in his own voice. They are far from painting a complete picture, even when supplemented by the diary of the lynx-eyed aunt who for a time lived in his house, for he is writing to a daughter who is eleven when the letters start and seventeen when they end and, until the last years, when the writer allows himself to take a couple of holidays and describes what he sees, they tell us more about the education of early Victorian girls than about the pre-occupations of a busy Calcutta doctor. We see him getting into his carriage promptly after breakfast but not where he goes. Nor do we catch more than an occasional side-view of the transformation of British India, with its annexations and modernisations, under the manic Governor-Generalship of Lord Dalhousie. It is essentially a family record; a record of separation at a time when pen and ink provided the only means of communication, when there was only one regular mail a month and when a letter took six weeks to travel between London and Calcutta. The framework and professional content of Dr Jackson's life must be supplied from elsewhere, as far as they can be supplied at all.

*　　　*　　　*

When John Jackson set out for Calcutta early in 1830, with his Cambridge degree and his Membership of the Royal College of Surgeons, the journey could well take six months. Macaulay, travelling

2

three years later, did it in four, which was considered a quick and easy passage. Within a decade everything was to be changed by steamships and railway trains, but nothing had changed yet: things seemed to be as they always had been. Since the answer to a letter could not be counted on within a year, the East India Company ran its three presidencies of Bengal, Bombay and Madras, with their connecting cats' cradle of allied native states, much as the men on the spot thought fit, subject to occasional guidance from its Directors in Leadenhall Street and a reluctant review by Parliament every twenty years when its Charter came up for renewal. Those who went out did not expect to come back in a hurry. Many did not come back at all; they died. Those who survived tended to marry late, usually a colleague's sister or daughter or widow, hoping to have made enough money to retire in time to rear their children at home before sending their sons back to repeat the pattern. Some stayed in India, with or more often without the Company's permission, striking root to some extent and often producing a family of half-Indian offspring for whom jobs (or husbands) in India would need to be found. At all levels there was a network of family connections, not only in the ruling castes of the Company's military and civil servants and the successful entrepreneurs, but also in the humbler world of seafarers, blacksmiths, coachbuilders, agents, auctioneers, book-keepers: all the innumerable trades and professions that combined to build Calcutta into a city that could be compared with the great commercial cities of Europe. It was from this humbler world that the Jacksons emerged.

John Jackson's father had been a 'Captain in the country trade', master of one of those ships licensed by the East India Company to trade with other parts of Asia, carrying cotton or sugar or silk or (behind the Company's back) opium from India and picking up and disposing of other cargoes as they went out and returned. If the Captain George Jackson who married in 1796 may be identified with the George Jackson who sailed from Calcutta to Canton as First Officer of the *Princess Royal* ten years earlier, he was a rather attractive character; quite sufficiently tough for a tough trade but with a taste for poetry, an ability to pick up and sing the tunes of songs heard on the way and

3

perhaps a livelier sense of responsibility both to his underlings and to his employer than could always be counted on.[4] Be that as it may, by the time he was thirty-eight he could afford to marry the sixteen-year-old Mary Howard, daughter of the 'Cryer and Apparitor' of the Bengal Supreme Court. Their first son was born in Calcutta at the turn of the century, but not long afterwards they shifted base to England and settled at Hackney. Here presumably the ex-Captain pursued his business interests and here in 1804 his second son, John, was born. By 1809 he had acquired a country address also, and it was at North Reston Hall, near Louth in north Lincolnshire, that his children grew up, their father an esquire. Many years later John's obituarist was to note, perhaps a shade defensively, that Dr Jackson was 'a thorough gentleman in every sense of the word.'[5]

The elder Jackson died suddenly, shooting at a burglar at two in the morning, when John was nineteen. It therefore fell to the Tutor of his Cambridge College to forward his application to join the Bengal Army as a surgeon. This Tutor, George Corrie, was the younger brother of Daniel Corrie, the Archdeacon of Calcutta, and he thought it worth noting that his candidate was related to the Archdeacon's wife. They were in fact cousins; their mothers were half-sisters. Mrs Corrie's mother, a Mrs Ellerton, was firmly rooted in Bengal - she had almost certainly been born there and was eventually to die there - but the Daniel Corries had made their way to north Lincolnshire to look up 'Aunt Jackson' and her family in 1815 when the future Archdeacon was in England on sick leave and, if only through Mrs Ellerton and Mrs Jackson who regularly corresponded, they probably kept in touch afterwards. They were a warm-hearted and hospitable pair and would have been more than ready to absorb the young surgeon into their circle when he arrived in Calcutta.

It was an interesting connection. Both Corrie brothers, the Indian chaplain and the Cambridge don, had grown up in Lincolnshire and were thus not aliens, but they were of different calibre from anyone John Jackson was likely to have encountered in his own village, or as he made his way up Louth grammar school. Both were able, well educated and notably successful in getting on to easy terms with

4

Daniel Corrie, Bishop of Madras, earlier Archdeacon of Calcutta

5

younger men. Both were shaped by, and perhaps did something to shape, the surge of evangelical Anglicanism associated with the name of Charles Simeon that poured out from Cambridge in the last decades of the eighteenth and first of the nineteenth centuries. The elder had been one of the best-loved and consequently most effective of the East India Company's missionary chaplains during the relatively brief period when chaplains were encouraged to missionary zeal: the usual view was that they were there to serve the Company's armed forces and should otherwise keep their heads down, on no account interfering with native customs or encouraging others to do so. The age of heroes and martyrs was over by the time John Jackson grew up: Simeon was no longer mocked and teased but revered at Cambridge, Daniel Corrie was no longer struggling in remote cantonments to establish churches and schools, rescue orphans and bring the military to repentance, but was supporting a series of Bishops (for they died one after the other) in a diocese that included Bombay and Madras, and indeed for a time also Australia, as well as Bengal. But the tide was still flowing strongly; evangelicalism was in the process of being absorbed into the Anglican establishment. Whether or not the Jackson parents had been swept up in the first wave of Indian missionary enthusiasm and raised their children accordingly, it would have been strange if their son had not taken something of the mould, first at Cambridge and then at Calcutta. There can be little doubt that the two Corrie brothers were key figures in his life.

A surgeon newly recruited to the Company's Bengal service might spend some time in Calcutta before he was posted, picking up a general idea of what went on. There were unfamiliar diseases to be recognised, rules of treatment to be adjusted or investigated (what worked with meat-fed Englishmen in a cool climate did not necessarily work with vegetarian Indians in a hot one), a new language or languages to be learned. Not unlike the chaplains, surgeons appointed primarily to serve the Company's armed forces had found themselves drawn much further and into much less well-defined territory. As far as the public health of the capital was anyone's concern, it was theirs. They ran the two main hospitals, the General (or Presidency) Hospital for Europeans and the Native Hospital for Indians, and the Eye Infirmary, and they supervised the scatter of government dispensaries for the poor, some of these more like cottage hospitals, with provision for inpatients and major surgical operations. They found themselves lecturing in the vernacular in the Hindu and Muslim Colleges, using Arabic for scientific terms and, with the Hindu bar on handling corpses, the carcasses of sheep to teach human anatomy. They also taught in the vernacular in a medical college set up in the 1820s to train Indians as what might now be called paramedics - surgeons were in short supply and the Company's Directors were urging economy - but not doing so very successfully. Finding the way about professionally and at the same time learning the preoccupations of the Archdeacon's circle - the need for more Bishops, the management of schools and the rival claims of English and the vernacular as the medium of instruction, the disturbing evidence that those taught to read in order to read the Scriptures were in fact reading Tom Paine's *Rights of Man*, the question whether clergymen should accept invitations to Government House if there was to be dancing (Mrs Ellerton was very severe about dancing), the unending problem of establishing the dividing line between chaplains who were paid from Indian revenues and missionaries who were paid by their respective societies: all this was a very different world from that in which most recruits to the Company's service had their first introduction to life in India.

From Calcutta, Jackson was sent off to join his Regiment (the 16th Foot, stationed at Saugor in central India) for the basic military training that every surgeon required. Even those who opted for a civilian rather than a military career would remain part of the army, posted where the military authorities thought fit, and liable to recall in case of need. His first important posting was to the civil station at Ghazipur, on the Ganges between Patna and Benares. From Ghazipur he was moved on a temporary basis to fill a gap at the much larger station of Howrah, just across the river from Calcutta. Between postings he probably returned to Calcutta to stay with his aunt, Mrs Ellerton. He was certainly in Calcutta in the spring of 1834, for in April of that year he and the Archdeacon nearly drowned in each other's

7

company. They were being rowed up river to look at a house that the Archdeacon was thinking of borrowing for the hot weather when their boat was overturned in a tidal wave, and after struggling to extricate themselves from the cabin they were left floundering in stormy water until they were picked up by a passing indigo planter, 'himself in some difficulties,' and taken to the Bishop's summer residence for dry clothes and transport home by land.[6] This may have been one of the last occasions on which they were together, for in the autumn the Archdeacon moved to Madras, as its first Bishop, and within two and a half years both he and Mrs Corrie were dead.

Between the death of his cousin and that of her husband, in January 1837, John Jackson married the eighteen-year-old Maria Pattle and entered into a new stage of life and a largely different world.

*   *   *

At thirty-three, Jackson was still an Assistant-Surgeon and thus on modest pay. So far he had scarcely had a chance of building up any supplementary private practice, if only because he had been moving about. But he may well have had private means. His father had made his Will at a time when his family was still increasing, and had not specified which child should have what; he had simply said that his property should be divided among them. The eldest son, who had taken Orders, was settled in the living of North Reston. A younger son became the owner of North Reston Hall and Lord of the Manor. It seems reasonable to suppose that John, who came between them, should have profited by the 'messuage in Calcutta.' Even so, in wooing Maria, or Mia as she was always called, he had aimed rather high. Her father, an eighteenth rather than a nineteenth century type, had entered the Company's service at seventeen (he was the son of a Director) and now, through seniority rather than merit, had reached almost the top of the list of 'Senior Merchants', as the higher civilian officials were still called: he was a member of the Board of Revenue in Calcutta. He was said to be the greatest liar in India, though perhaps this was in mistake for his brother; he was said to drink; he was probably unfaithful to his wife; there were rumours among some of his descendants of an Indian curse; it was all imprecise, but none of it creditable. His wife, Adeline, on the other hand was a figure of aristocratic romance. Her father, the Chevalier de l'Etang, had started his career as a page at Versailles and ended it breeding horses for the Bengal cavalry. It was believed by his descendants that he had been exiled to Pondicherry on account of too warm an admiration for Marie Antoinette (he was to be buried in India at the age of eighty-four with her miniature on his heart); it was also believed that Louis XVI would have made him a Marquis if only he had signed the papers on his table before he was overtaken by the Revolution.[7] A handsome, courteous man who knew everything there was to be known about horses, he had been captured by the English in some Indian skirmish in 1793 and, after running a riding school in Calcutta and then working for the Nawab of Oudh, had apparently settled down contentedly to help run the Company's studs and spend the rest of his life in British India.

Madame de l'Etang had other tastes. She left India in 1813, settling first in Paris and then at Versailles, playing whist, following the fashions and attending to the education first of her daughters and then of her granddaughters. Her daughters (Mrs Pattle and her two sisters) she sent to the grandest girls' school in France. It was established by the former Reader to Marie Antoinette and was where the new men, starting with the young Napoleon, sent their daughters and sisters to be turned into ladies. The aim of the school was said to be to produce good 'mères de famille' and the note struck was that princesses were treated just like anyone else. All pupils learned how to make soup for the poor, cut out and sew their own clothes and even wash their own lace, but they also sang and drew and acted and read a certain amount of literature: altogether a more enlightened education than fell to most girls of the time.[8] Madame de l'Etang's granddaughters were too late for the school (in London they were to be found a bit short on formal education) but they grew up in much the same tradition of *ancien régime* refinement and assurance, underpinned by a good deal of practical competence. With their spontaneity, their charming soft clothes (for they spurned both corsets and crinolines), the verve of

9

James & Adeline Pattle (née de L'Etang), 1818

some and the beauty of others, they must have returned to India with very different standards and expectations from most of the young ladies who flitted in and out of Calcutta society:[9] John Jackson can have met no-one at all like Mia either in Louth or in the circle of the Archdeacon. He was evidently bowled over. Writing after his death, Coventry Patmore told Mia that the only time he had seen his old friend depart from his usual 'exquisite moderation' was once when he spoke of her, which he did 'with the pure and tender pride of a young lover and in a strain of words like that of a practised and reticent Poet.'[10] If the Pattles had reservations - for a civil surgeon was hardly a catch - they may have reflected that there were still other daughters for whom husbands would need to be found and perhaps that after all John Jackson was not badly off[11].

Three of Mia's sisters were married at much the same time as herself, one the year before, two the year after.[12] The two elder sisters, Julia and Sara, married the two most eminent officials in Calcutta, each of them more than twenty years older than his bride. Charles Cameron, the husband of Julia, and Thoby Prinsep, the husband of Sara, stood one on each side of the divide between those who believe that there are universal standards that it is the duty of governments to promote and those who are sceptical about universal standards and think that governments should do what they can with things as they are. Cameron, a Benthamite London barrister, who had played English country house cricket with the future Governor General, Lord Auckland, and had been one of the few men Macaulay thought worth talking to in India, was in the van of those set on bringing Indian affairs into some sort of rational order. The Pattle ladies thought him omniscient; many of the Bengal officials thought him a hopeless visionary. Prinsep, like his father-in-law, came from an Indian background (his own father had been an early entrepreneur in the indigo industry and in the fabrication of chintz) and had entered the Company's service in his 'teens. He was now at the top of the Calcutta secretariat, and entirely out of sympathy with reforms encouraged by Whig governments in England. Emily Eden, sister of the Whig Lord Auckland, thought him a bore (she thought most people in India bores unless they were connected with her London world) but

India Law Commission.

Charles Cameron

12

Author of a Narrative of Political and Military Transactions of British India &c &c

Thoby Prinsep

13

the general view was that he was delightful, and he was to be much loved by the next generation. Both these men were, or soon would be, members of the Governor General's Council and thus at the peak of Calcutta's social pyramid. Henry Bayley, the husband of Mia's younger sister Louisa, was not quite up to this, though he would eventually become a Judge of the Calcutta Supreme Court, but he came from a family solidly established in the Bengal service and his foot was on the ladder. The sisters were a cohesive and affectionate lot and a man who married one of them might expect, geography permitting, to see a good deal of his in-laws.

The Jacksons started their married life back at Ghazipur. It was a pleasant station, said to have the best climate in India, and now that steamers went regularly up and down the Ganges it was not more than a few days' journey from Calcutta so that there was no sense of being cut off. Mia may have known the place already, for it was where her grandfather, the Chevalier, had settled. At eighty, he had long passed any normal retiring age but there was a Government stud-farm in the neighbourhood and he went on living where he had worked. Dr Jackson can hardly have failed to come across this picturesque old gentleman in his earlier time on the station; he may even have owed him his introduction to the Pattle family. Rose-water and attar were the local Ghazipur products, so the place was surrounded by rose-gardens; it was also in the middle of the poppy-growing country that produced opium. For a couple of years Jackson supplemented his civil surgeon's pay by employment as Post Master and Examiner of Opium, but lost the latter office as a result of 'improper packing of the Benares opium of 1837/8,'[13] not it seems a serious hitch in his career. He was presumably present in the autumn of 1837 when the Governor General inspected the opium warehouses, passing through Ghazipur as his enormous marching camp travelled at the rate of ten miles a day between Calcutta and Simla, but is unlikely to have taken part in any of the other festivities of the occasion, for the same week Mia produced her first baby, Adeline Maria. A son followed a year and ten months later and was called George Corrie. Jackson is said to have established an eye clinic (eyes, after wounds and fractures, were one of the medical

14

service's main preoccupations) but otherwise his period as civil surgeon was without event. By the end of 1840 the Jacksons were back in Calcutta, and at the beginning of 1841 Dr Jackson was appointed Third Assistant Surgeon at the Presidency Hospital with official quarters nearby. He was to remain in Calcutta for the rest of his Indian service.

*   *   *

The changes that had been in the air when Dr Jackson had first arrived in India eleven years before were now taking shape. Steamships sailed up and down the Red Sea, so that travellers prepared to put up with a good many changes of conveyance and an uncomfortable crossing of Egypt could do the journey in six weeks rather than six months. Mails were becoming more frequent and reliable, as well as quicker. British governments intervened more effectively in Indian affairs; Indians and Englishmen in India might more easily inform themselves about what went on in Europe. Macaulay had come and gone, Charles Cameron had come and stayed; there was a large body of orderly legislation ready to be brought into force at a suitable moment, and, more immediately, the campaign for the English language was as good as won. A vigorous rearguard action by those (like Thoby Prinsep) who thought that the advantage lay in operating through local, or at least Indian, languages had been defeated, largely by the dynamic young Highlander of the Scottish mission[14] (a friend of the Corries) who maintained that mastery of the English language in itself undermined the conceptual framework of Hinduism, thus opening the way to Christianity and modern science, and this line of thought was to be reinforced by Macaulay's observation that young Indians were ready to pay to be taught English but not to be taught Sanskrit. Indian and English entrepreneurs found that their interests largely coincided: modernisation, or Europeanisation, was the temper of the time. This note was caught by Emily Eden in the context of the dress expected at Government House in 1836. Hitherto Indians had been required to take off their shoes when they came in, as was indeed the

15

THE RIGHT HONORABLE GEORGE EARL OF

Auckland

G.C.B. &c

The Earl of Auckland, Governor-General, 1834-42

general practice in Bengal. But 'there is a large class here who think the natives sufficiently well-informed to feel the degradation very sensibly, and to wish the natives to adopt European manners as much as possible', she wrote. 'George [the Governor General] has taken up that opinion',[15] and Indians henceforward might go to Government House shod like Englishmen.

The decisive battle for Europeanisation had been won on the eve of Macaulay's arrival. A Committee appointed to look into medical education had recommended that the existing medical college should be wound up and replaced by an institution on far more ambitious lines. It should be open to all Indians, without distinction of caste or creed, with rigorous standards both at entry and at the end of the course; it should lay down a foundation of general scientific knowledge to support hospital-based medical training (this was a largely new idea) and it should teach throughout in English. The aim would be to produce medical practitioners with qualifications recognised by such examining bodies as the Surgeons or the Apothecaries of London. The Committee reported at the end of 1834. Its recommendations were promptly accepted. By the summer of 1835 the new College had come into existence with its first eleven pupils (five were to complete the course successfully) and its tiny, pioneering staff. The next year a Hindu instructor broke through caste rules to dissect a human body. The significance of this event was recognised by a salute of guns from Fort William and the horrified retreat of an eminent Brahmin from the polluted city.[16]

The foundation subjects (chemistry, botany, and anatomy), could be taught in the College's existing premises without difficulty, but when it came to experience at the bedside it was a very different matter. Students were given access to the existing hospitals, but the General Hospital (for Europeans) was more than two miles away and the Native Hospital, though nearer, catered only for very limited categories of patient: it was a charitable foundation picking up the very poor, and it dealt with surgical cases only. After a year's experience, with students wasting much time going to and fro and probably some difficulty in fitting them into existing routines, a strong case was put up for

NATH. WALLICH. M.D. F.R.S.

Professor of Botany.

Medical College Calcutta.

Med: Jour! Press. Fort William.

Nathaniel Wallich, the learned Dane,
one of the founding fathers of the Calcutta Medical College

H.H. GOODEVE ESQ⁺ᵉ M.D.
Professor of Anatomy and Medicine.
Medical College. Calcutta.
Med. Jour. Press. Fort William.

*H.H. Goodeve, one of the College's founding fathers, who in 1839 brought four
successful students to England to obtain their MRCS at University College London*

19

establishing a large general hospital specifically attached to the Medical College, with its clinical wards 'exclusively under the College Professors' (thus under civil rather than military authority, for the College fell within the province of the Board of Education). This was approved, as promptly as the Governor General's absence in Simla permitted, in September 1838. Meanwhile, until plans for the big hospital could be worked out and brought into effect there would be a small, rather makeshift, hospital attached to the College and under its general administration; and it is a pretty safe guess that when Dr Jackson was transferred from Ghazipur to a post in Calcutta it was with the needs of this embryonic College Hospital in mind.

For teaching staff were the central problem. They had to be rustled up from those at hand. Not many doctors in India had academic qualifications and those that had were likely to be committed to their careers in the army. The two senior 'professors' were the learned Dane, Dr Nathaniel Wallich, already a Fellow of the Royal Society, who was in charge of the Botanic Gardens and the Superintendent of the Eye Hospital; otherwise posts were filled, at first rather provisionally and chaotically, by vigorous army surgeons in their thirties, almost all educated at Edinburgh, who were prepared to turn their hand to anything. Dr Jackson's Cambridge Bachelor of Medicine degree might not be up to an Edinburgh Doctorate but it was something. He had been highly thought of by the College of Surgeons in London, he had done well so far in India and as a civil surgeon he was available. Since the affairs of the Medical College passed through the hands of three of Mia's brothers-in-law (Henry Bayley then acting as assistant secretary in the Home Department, Charles Cameron Chairman of the Board of Education, Thoby Prinsep the senior official who put papers before the Governor General), his qualifications were unlikely to be either overlooked or misjudged. As soon as he was back in Calcutta he was invited to complete the course of lectures on surgery interrupted by the Professor's furlough, and in the summer he was appointed to the post of Professor of Medicine and Clinical Medicine in the College, thus in charge of the clinical side of the new little hospital.

This was one of two key appointments made in the same year. The other was that of Resident Secretary and Treasurer (in effect Principal) of the Medical College.[17] This post went to an Assistant Surgeon called Mouat who had come to the notice of the Bengal Government through his negotiations with the Liverpool Chamber of Commerce over the use of lichens as dye stuffs. He subsequently invented an improved percussion cap for the artillery, he was Professor successively of Chemistry, Medical Jurisprudence and (after Dr Jackson), Clinical Medicine, he served as Secretary to the Bengal Committee of Education and provided it with a whole scheme for higher education in Bengal. This whirlwind of a man, who knew precisely how he thought everything should be done, and kept an eye on everything that went on in the hospital, was ten years junior to Dr Jackson in the service and relations between them may occasionally have been awkward. If so, it was not allowed to affect pupils or patients or the development of the College as a whole. The students regarded both with respect[18] (Dr Jackson also it seems with affection), the hospital's mortality figures, whether for Indian or for European patients, if marginally worse than those of St Bartholomew's Hospital in London were better than those of St George's or of the Great Hospital of Milan or the Imperial Hospital of Vienna, with fewer doctors,[19] and by the middle 'forties the College's certificates were recognised by London and Edinburgh and its Professors included among the first Fellows to be elected by the London College of Surgeons. The whole thing had been done within a decade.

*   *   *

If all had gone well with the children, those first years in Calcutta might have been the happiest of the Jacksons' lives. Mia, with the resources of the capital at her disposal, was once more surrounded by her sisters. The three married sisters were all in or near Calcutta already and it was not long before Mrs Pattle brought the two youngest back from a period in Europe so that for a time - and for the last time - the family (with its swarm of new babies) was complete. Dr Jackson had all the stimulus of working in the growing College with colleagues as vigorous and intelligent as any group in Calcutta and, with his position in the new little teaching hospital and his substantive post in the Presidency Hospital, was in the way of acquiring an unusually thorough acquaintance with Indian diseases and their management. Both personally and professionally he was well set on a prosperous career and indeed (to anticipate), he achieved it. In 1845 he left the Presidency Hospital to become Surgeon-in-charge of the Native Hospital and in 1849 he was promoted Presidency Surgeon (the equivalent of Lt Colonel), the highest point a civil surgeon could reach and generally considered a passport to a flourishing and remunerative private practice. The course could hardly have been more smooth.

But that first Calcutta autumn little George Corrie died, a few days after his second birthday. Another child, Mary Louisa, was born some three months later; but nothing could be entirely golden again. The early 'forties were a bad time for health. There was more cholera in Calcutta than usual, and there was a lot of measles and smallpox about as well. It was impossible not to be anxious. During the hot weather of 1844 first Mia and then Adeline fell ill, and in September Dr Jackson hastily packed off wife and daughters to England. Thoby Prinsep had retired the year before and was now settled in London, applying himself (unsuccessfully) to becoming a Member of Parliament, so that he and Sara would be able to look after them and might take charge of the children when Mia returned.

At this point Mrs Ellerton, Dr Jackson's aunt, reappears on the scene. She had been with the Corries in Madras, and after the death of her daughter and son-in-law had looked after a granddaughter until she married. She was now very much on her own, and so far without a permanent lodging in. Calcutta. The Lord would provide, she gaily declared, as she moved from one set of friends to another. When her nephew suggested that she should come and live in his house while Mia was away, she accepted with alacrity. He was a son to her, she told a friend,[20] and now that her immediate family were dead or dispersed it was on him and his children that her affections were to be concentrated. (She was liable to drop in unexpectedly, sometimes at awkward moments, as when Mia was having a warm bath to mitigate the effects of a riding accident.) At seventy-two, she was one of those wiry indefatigable little women who sit on committees and organize charity bazaars, her natural capacity for enjoyment battened down under her puritanical principles, and she was a little touchy about her social position. Growing up in the household of her stepfather, the Supreme Court official, she had watched the Calcutta grandees all her life (as a child of eight in 1780 she had seen Philip Francis carried off in a stretcher after his duel with Warren Hastings), her first husband, Mrs Corrie's father, had been one of the early Trustees of the Calcutta Evangelical Fund, so that she had known all the great missionaries of the first part of the century, her second, Mr Ellerton, a prosperous indigo planter, had moved in much the same world, setting up Christian schools and translating the New Testament into Bengali. When her son-in-law became Archdeacon her acquaintance widened further to include almost everyone of importance in Calcutta. She felt that now she was alone she had somehow lost caste and she was pleased to be brought back into the swim by her nephew. She liked the connection with the Prinseps; she liked going as a matter of course to the christening of the latest Cameron baby, with John Jackson as godfather; Charles Cameron, as senior member of the Council, took the Governor General's place when he was away and Julia, not yet thirty, flung herself into the role of First Lady. But she did not approve of the Pattles. 'Proud', she thought they were, and she mistrusted their background as worldly and lacking in seriousness. 'I fear the effect of French education', she noted in her diary when she discovered that Mia was having singing lessons. Fond as Dr Jackson was of her, she was not likely to be an entirely easy lodger.

Mia did not linger in England. Tearing herself away from her two little daughters, left in the Prinseps' charge, she travelled back by the new quick route via Egypt and was in Calcutta again in April 1845.

At about the same time there was a change in Dr Jackson's position. He left his post at the Presidency Hospital on appointment as Surgeon to the Native Hospital, moving up from official quarters in the military area beyond Fort William to a house in the grand Chowringhee

Road that looked over the open space of the Maidan towards the river. This step up the career ladder released him from the peripheral duties connected with the Calcutta Native Militia and the Calcutta Jail that had gone with the earlier post and perhaps widened his acquaintance with what his obituarist was to call 'natives of the highest classes.' The patients might come from the dregs of the city's population, but the Indians on the Committee of Management - for the hospital was a charitable foundation - would have been drawn from the world of wealthy landholders, bankers and entrepreneurs, active in local good causes, among whom he was to move with some ease. That he was largely accepted into this world, even to the extent of 'gaining admission to the houses of Indian Ranees,' was to be remembered long after he had left India.

More immediately, the posting plunged him into one of the exercises that interested him most in his professional career, consideration of 'mesmerism' as a means of controlling pain in surgery.[21] This was professionally a bold enterprise. In the English medical establishment the use of mesmerism was anathema. The term was stretched to cover not only the creation of a trance-like or somnambulistic state in the patients but almost anything to do with the operation of the mind, from phrenology to clairvoyance, and was regarded as a retreat from scientific method into magic and chicanery. It was

'Farewell to the Hall and farewell to the College
Farewell to chirugico-medical knowledge,'

as one of the livelier contributors to *The Lancet* put it: a 'contagion worse than leprosy,' as another wrote.[22] Only a few years before, a London professor of Clinical Medicine had been obliged to resign from his hospital post for taking its therapeutic possibilities seriously.[23] But now a civil surgeon up the river at Hooghly, Esdaile by name, had produced evidence that it was difficult to ignore. In his local 'dispensary' he had been using mesmerism not only in medical, but also in a large number and variety of surgical, cases with conspicuous success. No-one, beyond a dentist whose experience was brushed aside, had tried this in England. To any surgeon trained to operate with no anaesthetics beyond alcohol or opium - and every European doctor in India was primarily a surgeon - a procedure that might expedite an operation, eliminate or diminish pain, reduce shock, and thus possibly save life, was worth taking seriously. A committee was accordingly set up to advise the Bengal Government whether Esdaile's work should be pursued. It was a high-powered and wide-ranging body, consisting of three lay members (one of them the police magistrate) and four doctors. The Chairman was the Inspector General of Hospitals who had published a pioneering (but largely disregarded) treatise on treating stones in the bladder but was primarily known as a translator of Persian poetry and one of the leading Orientalists of his day. The Secretary was one of the founding fathers of the Medical College and its first Professor of Chemistry, and was now in the process of introducing the electric telegraph to India. The other two doctors were Dr Jackson and the Professor of Midwifery. This group considered the cases of ten volunteer patients in a ward of the Native Hospital set aside for the purpose.

It was a pretty inconclusive experiment. Three of the volunteers proved immune to hypnotism. In another three cases the results were said to be doubtful. In four cases however, one of them an amputation at the hip, operations were carried out without pain. This result was considered good enough to warrant a year's public funding of a 'mesmeric hospital' in which Esdaile would continue his work. The hospital did not last long. At the end of the following year the Professor of Clinical Surgery at University College Hospital in London carried out the first operation under ether, declaring at the end 'This Yankee dodge beats mesmerism hollow,'[24] and a year after that James Simpson in Edinburgh established the anaesthetic properties of chloroform, used it successfully for an amputation five days later and immediately published the results. The news travelled fast. Already in their 1847-8 Reports the more enterprising local hospitals in India were noting successful use of chloroform, once or twice of ether, and although 'mesmerists' continued to perform here and there, mesmerism as a subject of serious research was dead.[25]

While the experiment was in progress, James Pattle died (of drink, it was said), leaving instructions that he was to be buried in England. Off the body went, preserved in a cask of rum (or, in one version, brandy) on a journey that was to attract macabre legends faithfully transmitted to his descendants, but apparently quite groundless. Poor Mrs Pattle, who went home with the two youngest daughters at the same time, died on the journey leaving Virginia and Sophie, now eighteen and sixteen, to arrive in England alone. They were duly scooped up by the Prinseps and taken to join their little nieces at 9 Chesterfield Street, the house between Berkeley Square and Park Lane that was in the process of becoming the Pattle family base. To this house, a few weeks later, Dr Jackson wrote the first of the many letters that his eldest daughter was to keep all her life.

Calcutta, Feb 8 1846

My dearest Addy

I must write to you and to darling Mary Loo, to let you know that you have both got another little Sister, and that it arrived yesterday at 4 o'clock. It is a very fine and pretty looking Baby, more like Addy than Mary Loo, and is a very good little Child doing nothing but sleep, never has been known to cry. What we shall call this little Sister I can not tell you but I think we shall call it Julia after your dear Aunt, whom we all love so much. How I wish that you and sweet Mary Loo were with us or that we were with you in London: but when that will be I cannot tell, but hope it may come some happy time when I may put you both on my knee, as Uncle Thoby [Prinsep] now does. Give my love to Aunt Sarah & to Virginia & Sophy and tell them that they must all give you a kiss from their Mamma and tell Aunty Sarah that we miss her so much & that we should so have liked Aunty Virginia to have been here that she might have nursed the little Baby and have been with your darling Mamma who is now in bed, & is unable to write and tell you about Baby but she will do next mail & have much more to tell you than I can. Give sweet Mary Loo a thousand Kisses from her dear Papa - and now goodbye, dearest darling Addy.
 Your fond Papa
 J. Jackson.

Adeline and Mary Jackson in England

When it came to the point the Jacksons felt that Prinseps as well as Julia Cameron should be recognised in the naming of their new daughter and she was accordingly christened Julia Prinsep. This was the daughter who was to marry Leslie Stephen and become the mother of the painter Vanessa Bell, Virginia Woolf and the only one of the Jacksons' twelve grandsons to qualify as a doctor.

References

1. A. Bell (Ed.). *Sir Leslie Stephen's Mausoleum Book*, Oxford 1977, pp.25-28.
2. B. Champneys. *Coventry Patmore*, London 1900, II, pp.215-216.
3. H.A.L. Fisher. *Unfinished Autobiography*, Oxford 1940, pp.12-13.
4. A. Bulley. *Free Mariner*, BACSA 1992, pp.54-142. My only doubt about the identification of the First Officer in 1786 with the Captain of 1796 is that the former was said to come from Lancashire (crew list p. 54). But "Lancashire" may have been a mishearing or misreading of "Lincolnshire."
5. The *B.M.J.* 1887 I contains two obituaries (p.914 and p.1249) the latter apparently a revised version of the former. The quotation is from the former. I suspect the influence of Mrs Jackson in the latter.
6. *Memoirs of Bishop Corrie edited by his Brothers*, London 1847, p.566.
7. John Beaumont's researches in the French archives have now established the facts, as distinct from the family mythology, of the Chevalier's background. (See *Virginia Woolf Bulletin*, nos.7 & 8 2001, "The Chevalier de L'Etang (1757-1840) and his descendants, the Pattles" by John Beaumont)
8. *Journal Anecdotique de Mme de Campan*, Paris 1834. cf C. Colvin (Ed.). *Maria Edgeworth in France and Switzerland*, Oxford 1979, pp.32, 40.
9. They were not universally approved, any more than they were later to be approved by London Society. The daughter of the Commander-in-Chief thought Sara (Mrs Prinsep) "nasty," with "nonsensical airs and graces," while Julia (later Mrs Cameron) "sets up for a bas-bleu... so ugly and conceited withal." J.C. Pemble (Ed.). *Miss Fane in India*, London 1985, pp.39, 61, 99.
10. B. Champneys op cit
11. An Assistant Surgeon, not in any case likely to rank as a gentleman at this date, remained on the same pay until he was promoted Surgeon, probably after more than fifteen years service and certainly on seniority rather than merit. A civil surgeon had little prospect of being shifted sideways into an administrative post (as military surgeons occasionally were) and none of reaching the top of the Medical Service with an Inspectorate. In Bengal the highest post open to him was that of Presidency Surgeon, in effect general practitioner to the Calcutta officials, usually with some superintendence of a dispensary or charitable institution, membership of various Government Committees and as much private practice as he cared to take on. D.G. Crawford. *History of Indian Medical Service*, London 1914, II, pp.269 ff (for Dalhousie's ferocious 1856 criticism of the organisation of the Medical Service).
12. The eldest of the Pattle sisters, Adeline, died the year before the Jackson marriage, on her way home with her three little daughters. She had been married to an officer in the Madras army, Colin Mackenzie (later Major General).
13. IOR: L/MIL/10/71. This record of Dr. Jackson's service, copied by a rather confused clerk, suggests that there was a penal element in his ceasing to be Opium Examiner "and to be attached to the civil station at Ghazipur." This can hardly be, since the move to Calcutta in 1840 was clearly a step up.

14. Dr. Alexander Duff. cf. G.E. Smith: *Life of Dr. Duff*, London 1879. I pp.178ff

15. E. Eden. *Letters from India*, London 1872, I, p.116.

16. Crawford op cit. II pp.435 ff for the history of the Medical School and Hospital.

17. The embryonic Medical College Hospital had been opened in April 1838, apparently with some beds but also, and probably primarily, with a dispensary for outpatients. It is hard to believe that it was fully operational before 1841 when a number of new appointments were made besides the two mentioned, and the post of Professor of Medicine and Clinical Medicine, left vacant for three years, was again filled.

18. IOR: L/MIL/24719.

19. The mortality figures are those for 1841-53, quoted in the *Annual Report of the Medical College of Bengal* for 1852-3, pp.9-10. IOR: V/24/4478.

20. Letter to Mrs. Alexander Duff, quoted by Smith op cit II p.109

21. Crawford op cit, II pp.153-156

22. *The Lancet*, 1946 I, pp.164, 687. *The Lancet* for 1845 and 1846 offers very entertaining and informative reading on mesmerism.

23. Dr. John Elliotson, to whom Thackeray was to dedicate *Pendennis*.

24. Quoted by D. Guthrie. *History of British Medicine*, London 1945, p.307. The surgeon was R. Liston.

25. IOR: V/24/736 *Half-yearly reports of the Government Charitable Dispensaries*, Calcutta 1849.

Country Hospital Ward

2

Separation

(i) 1848-1849

In March 1848 Mia took Julia to England. It was three years since she had seen her two elder daughters, now ten and six, and at two Julia had reached an age when cautious parents started to think about transferring their children to Europe. But it seems likely that the decision was precipitated by Mia's own health. She had again been ill; very ill, it seems, though what form the illness took is not recorded. In 1844 the sea voyage and change of scene had put her on her feet and sent her back to India recovered; it was reasonable to hope that the same would happen again. Charles Cameron had just retired, so that she could travel under his and her sister's care, with every expectation that she would arrive in England a good deal better than when she started and would be back in Calcutta in a matter of months.

It turned out otherwise. Mia was severely crippled with rheumatic pains. A period of trying one health resort after another followed - seaside towns on the south coast, Malvern, where there was a doctor approved by Mrs Prinsep, Leamington, where there was a fashionable water cure, Spa in Belgium. For most of the time she kept her three little girls with her; occasionally Adeline was sent off for a brief visit to an aunt. It may be that old Madame de l'Etang intervened from time to time, making sure that her great-grandchildren at least learnt French properly. Perhaps they were occasionally sent off to her at Versailles, with attendant nurses and governesses; certainly she turned up every now and then at 9 Chesterfield Street, for on one occasion in the late 'forties when the painter GF Watts called he was startled to find her on all fours, playing with the Prinseps' little boys.[1] This Chesterfield Street house must have seemed their real home to Addy and Mary Jackson, with Uncle Thoby and Aunt Sara and Aunt Virginia Pattle, still unmarried, their permanent grownups; and it remains one of the two fixed points in the confusing family movements of the next couple of years.

The other fixed point was 14 Chowringhee Road, Dr Jackson's house in Calcutta. However ill Mia might be, there was no question of his joining her in England. Even leaving aside his own professional commitments, the second Sikh war was being fought and all civil surgeons were pinned down in reserve. His house was large, and in accordance with the usual practice of Anglo-India he was expected to provide friends and relations with lodging and a common table as need might arise. His aunt, Mrs Ellerton, had already dug in as a permanent resident. She seems to have taken on some household chores, such as dealing with the laundry bills, and she was sometimes, though not invariably, invited out to dinner when her nephew was, but on the whole she lived an independent life, with her own lady's maid, her 'own little carriage,' her own large circle of friends and her own church-based activities. She helped to manage one or two of Calcutta's schools (not hesitating to let a master know when she found his drawing-room too grand for his station), and she devoted much time and energy to the Asylum, an orphanage where little girls, theoretically European but probably often of mixed race, were given a Christian upbringing and either trained for domestic service or sent on to other schools, perhaps with a view to becoming governesses or missionary teachers. Whenever she felt unwell, as she often did, she summoned her nephew upstairs to prescribe as soon as he came back from his rounds, whether it was a headache (leeches), spasms (twenty drops of ether, or simply 'stillness and repose'), or swollen throat (iodine painted on and quinine swallowed) and she noted every fluctuation of his manner to herself. One day he might meet her 'very affectionately at breakfast,' on another he was 'distant and cool.' Was he getting tired of her? Her greatest pleasure was in their rare tête-à-tête dinners and evenings, when he might read aloud an article in the *Calcutta Review* while she 'wound off thread.' They were both lonely, and though he may occasionally have found her maddening it was probably a real comfort to have her there.

31

The other long-term, though not permanent, lodgers were Mia's youngest sister, Sophie Dalrymple, with her husband and fragile first baby. This was an awkward combination. The Dalrymples were young and unusually good-looking, perhaps rather spoilt and off-hand, and they liked parties and balls. Mrs Ellerton liked parties too, within reason, but was quite happy to settle for 'a nice long talk on the doings of God' with a friend, followed by a joint excursion to the burial ground to inspect 'my grave that is to be.' She felt that the Dalrymples regarded her as an 'eye-sore,' as they very likely did, and that they treated her 'like some old nurse supported on the family's charity.' John Dalrymple she thought the rudest man she had ever met, his regular failure to offer her his arm when they all went down to dinner giving particular offence. She was to reach a point when she found herself creeping up the back stairs or lurking in her nephew's room on the ground floor in order to avoid meeting them in the drawing-room when she came in late.[2] Scrupulous as she doubtless was in confining her feelings to her diary, Dr Jackson may have noticed nothing amiss. If he did, he decided in favour of silence; he was rather fond of his young in-laws, and certainly amused by them. Other lodgers, unnamed, who passed through more briefly, may have provided some padding. It can hardly have been comfortable, but calm was preserved.

The first of Dr Jackson's regular letters to his eldest daughter (or perhaps the first that she kept) dates from the end of 1848, just after Adeline's eleventh birthday, when the family was at Brighton. He wrote in the first week of almost every month, very rapidly and without correction or erasure. Openings varied; 'My dearest Addy,' 'My dearest child Adeline,' 'My very dear child.' But the end was always the same. He was 'Ever your fond Papa.'

Calcutta Dec[r] 7 1848
I have received your letters of 23rd September and the 6th October and am very sorry to find you have been unwell, ... Now I must give you a little trouble perhaps, and ask you to look out for a Map of India, and in the North West portion of it to find out the Punjab, or the country of the 5 Rivers, and at the Southern & Eastern Corner of it to look for the

City of Moultan. At this present time there is a War in this city and the King of the City who is called Moolraj has no Silver money to pay his soldiers, & has only Gold and he gives to each of his soldiers every month 5 and six little Gold Coins which are equal to half a crown each. I have sent you one of the little Gold Coins, which I received yesterday in a letter from a little Nephew of mine who is with the Army.[3] It is quite a curiosity this Gold Coin, and I am sure that you will take care of it, and keep it with your other little presents...

*   *   *

Calcutta 8th Jan[y] 1849
Your Mamma has sent me by your Aunt Sophie's Box, a little packet of your School Exercises which has interested me very much, and I have been very glad to find that Miss Barton has adopted such a nice Method of causing you to think and to express yourself in writing and perhaps when you make any little journey you will be able to send me an account of what you see, for you know dear Addy that I am always so delighted to receive your letters and to observe the progress you make. Your darling Mamma tells me that she is a little stronger so that I hope before she leaves Brighton that she will be able to take a walk with you. How happy I shall be when I can hear that darling Mamma is quite well... I am sorry to hear that you have been obliged to have a Tooth taken out, and that it should have been on my Birthday, but you must have forgotten all the pain soon, for your Mamma tells me that you always behave very well. Next mail I shall expect to receive from you the Hymn from Milton which your Mamma says you were learning by heart and that you would write it out from Memory and send it to me. Tell little Julia that next month Mrs Ellerton is sending her a little Box of letters and I now send her a kiss and must ask you dear Addy to give it to her with her Papa's fond love.

*   *   *

[Undated, probably spring 1849]
... I have not heard in any of your late letters how you have been getting on in your Music, & whether you like the Piano. Your French lessons can no longer be a task to you now, for I expect that you are able to write

33

Sophie Dalrymple

Hannah Ellerton

35

and speak French as well as you can English. Your Aunt Sophy [Dalrymple] are [sic] pretty well, but Baby is not yet able to walk or sit up, without being supported, and it continues very small. It goes out in the Carriage with Aunt Sophy every Evening, and the Nurse takes him for a walk in the morning. I suppose your little sister Julia runs about on the sands and is very happy. Give her a kiss from me & may God bless you my own dear Child.

*   *   *

[Undated, probably spring 1849]
... A few Mails ago I sent to your Mamma a Picture done by the Photograph. Did you remember it Addy, & think it at all like what you recollect of me, I suppose you can only very slightly remember me. We must try to keep each other in recollection by writing every month and then you will feel I hope that your Papa is very fond of you. Have you begun to learn Chess Addy, if not you must ask your Mamma to give you with my love a set of Chess Men and a Board, & you must ask her to teach you the game. You will find it very Interesting and it will teach you Attention and enable you to think & reflect. You will be able to teach Mary too after a little time. I hope to hear that your darling Mamma has become stronger and that she is able to walk out.

*   *   *

[Undated, but 28 May 1849]
...During the last week there has been much gaiety in Calcutta an accompaniment of Entertainment given to Lord Gough who is going to England by the first steamer[4] - Sir Laurence Peel[5] gave him a large Party at which were several illustrations with the names of the several Countries in which he had been engaged as Commander-in-Chief and where he had great victories Sabraon China Gwalior the Punjab, the whole was very tastefully got up and when seen at night in a beautiful garden the Effect was very pretty. Your Aunts Louisa [Bayley] and Sophy [Dalrymple] went to the Ball. Today the Lord Gough went by Steamer to England. Now every one seems to be going to England & why cannot I go. I sometimes think dear Addy of my need to go & see your darling Mamma & see all of you & perhaps next March four years

36

General Gough

37

I shall be able to do so but this is too long a time to think forward to & we will therefore fix no time. I hope that little Addy Bayley and her sister are very well. Her Mamma is often talking about them and has a little picture of Addy . It is a pretty picture but I like the one of you much better. When you next see Mr Watts you must tell him how very much obliged I am for all the kind trouble he has taken. The picture of your dear Mamma is most beautiful, & so it should be to be like should it not dear Addy.

There is now a gap in Dr Jackson's letters. 1849 was the year in which, with his promotion to Presidency Surgeon, he gave up the Professorship at the Medical College, with its responsibilities at the Medical College Hospital, and he may have been through a time of particular pressure; but it seems more likely that his letters were lost in the confusion of his family's movements in England than that he failed to write them. By the end of the summer Mia, after experimenting with Hastings and Tunbridge Wells, was with her children at Malvern.

> Calcutta Nov 7 1849
> Friday week darling Addy will be your Birthday. I send you my fond love and many happy returns of that day. They will make me happy I am sure when I am able to come home and enjoy it with you and dear Mamma & your sisters...
> I hope you will be able to make little sketches about Malvern. Your Mamma has sent me some of your first sketches, & these I shall keep very carefully, & when I come home I shall bring them with me. I have sent you by the present steamer a little Scarf to put round your neck. It is not so pretty as I should have liked, but it will remind you of dear Papa & I hope will keep you warm in the cold weather. Your Aunt Sophy's Baby is a little better, and has become somewhat stronger, but he is still very weak, and is not able to walk or crawl. She is very fond of him and gives up all her mornings to the care of her little Boy.

References

1. M. Watts. *Life of G.F. Watts*, I p.129
2. Mrs. Ellerton's diary for this period does not survive, but she harks back to her grievance in later notebooks, notably in August 1854, when she was feeling sorry for herself after a feverish cold.

3. Unless the Lt. George Jackson of the 4th Regt. Light Cavalry (the Lancers) was the son of James Lewis Jackson, Dr. Jackson's illegitimate half-brother named in the elder George Jackson's Will, the "little nephew" must have been a sister's son. There were nine legitimate Jacksons, of whom the eldest brother, the Vicar of North Reston, seems to have had no surviving son and the younger, who inherited the North Reston estate, none at this stage. I have not attempted to track down the sisters or any other possible brothers.

4. Lord Gough, 1779-1869, went from Madras to command in Canton in 1841. He became Commander-in-Chief in 1843 and commanded in both Sikh wars (1845 and 1848-9), finally defeating the Sikhs at the battle of Gujerat in February 1849. He left for home on May 28th 1849.

5. Sir Lawrence Peel, 1790-1884 (a first cousin of the statesman Robert Peel), was Chief Justice 1842-1855 and a patient of Dr. Jackson's. He was said to give away the whole of his substantial official salary.

Palkee carriage (converted palanquin)

39

(ii) 1850-1851

During the winter of 1849-50 it must have become clear that there was no immediate prospect of Mia's return to India. She was still very much an invalid. Plans were revised. She would spend an extra year in England and then return to India for a final year, after which both Jacksons would return to England for good. Meanwhile she and the children had moved from Malvern to Leamington.

Dr Jackson's letter of February 1850, catching up rather belatedly on Christmas (he was to remember in better time in the following years, with similar instructions about presents), was written on paper illustrated with romantic pictures of troubadours and ladies looking down from casements, highly suitable for a correspondent of thirteen. This set of stationery held out for the next three months.

> 7th Feb 1850
>
> How glad I should have been to have passed my Christmas with you all, I should have enjoyed so much to have seen you happy... I now enclose for you some money and must tell you what you are to do with it. You are to spend 2 Sovereigns upon a little present for Mamma which you are to give with Papa's love, and then you are to keep one Sovereign for yourself, and to spend it as you like best and you are to give Ten Shillings to Mary Loo, and the same to little Julia, and to give One Sovereign to old Nurse Byers and tell her that Papa has sent it to her as a Christmas Box. I have enclosed a little leaf meant for Baby, it flew into my Carriage the other day when I was driving with your Aunt Louisa [Bayley]. It is not very pretty, but if you put it under a Microscope I daresay it will look like the wings of a fly and will amuse you. So you are [reading] Joyce's Scientific Dialogues with Mamma, and I daresay you will soon read Mrs Marcet's Books on the same subject.[1] When dear Mamma is able to go out, I hope she will take Julia and Mary Loo, to one of the Infant Schools, where the lessons are all sung, and the different lines, and angles, explained most simply...

*　　　*　　　*

40

Calcutta March 8th 1850

I had almost feared I should have been unable to have answered your nice long letter, & have thanked you for the piece of Cowper's poetry which you have written out for me so well from Memory. The letters came in yesterday morning and I was suffering from a bad cold with headache but it has all passed off today and I am very well again. Yesterday the Governor General Lord Dalhousie arrived in Calcutta,[2] & the Troops were all paraded & the Guns fired Two Salutes, and Calcutta People all out to witness the arrival of the Governor General who has all the same respect paid to him in this Country, as the Queen of England has at home. Lady Dalhousie was there also, but she is not so courteous or condescending as the Queen, and is not very much liked. Your Uncle Henry [Bayley] and Uncle John [Dalrymple] were there, and a very large assemblage.

…I hope that if you all remain at Leamington another year or 10 months that your Mamma will be strong enough to return to India with your Aunt Sophy whom we all expect will go home at the end of the year, & your Mamma can return with her… and you will have the Happiness of having her another Year with you, & she will come back again with me after One Year & then I hope we shall all be happy together and have no more separations.

*　　　*　　　*

[8 April 1850]

... I hope you will have no more face ache & do not require any more Teeth to be taken out; for I know how painful a thing it is. I am very glad to find you bore it so well. It is always necessary to try to bear pain as well as you can, and not give way. By the time this reaches you, the pleasant mild weather will have come and then I hope darling Mamma will have gained some strength and have lost her suffering. It must be very distressing to see her confined to her couch as she is so constantly, tho I am quite sure Addy that you do all in your power to comfort her and that you give as little trouble as you possibly can. I am glad to find you like your dancing and Music lessons and that you are all keeping so well... Your Aunt [Sophie] is very well and we often have a long talk about you. I have got your picture and keep it always near me, so that I have you frequently in mind and always in recollection.

41

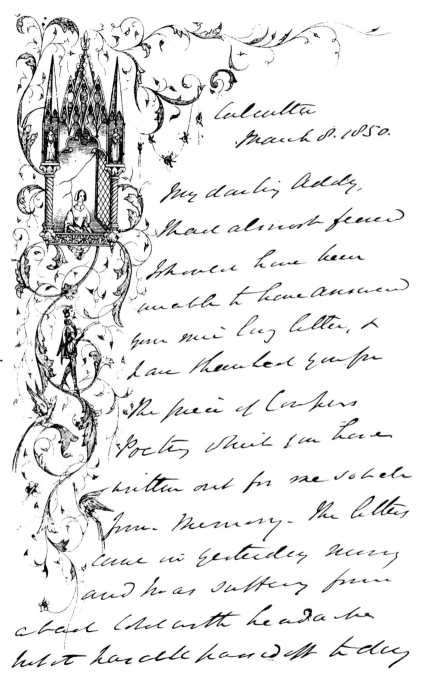

Facsimile of letter from Dr Jackson of 8 March 1850

*   *   *

Calcutta May 2 1850

How very pleasant the Weather is now with you I daresay my darling Addy, but in Calcutta it is very very hot and our May is very different from yours in England. Still we are all very well, and try to keep ourselves cool with Ice and the Punkah. To our great surprise the Steamer arrived two days ago and brought me your letter with others from Mamma & from Mary. I was very glad to find that you had received my February Letter safely and to learn that my present to old Bo, pleased you all so much... Only three years now Addy & then I hope to be with you all and to be enjoying a Trip through England with you all. I hope you have continued your dancing lessons & that you have made some sketches of Warwick Castle & other pretty places about Leamington. I have got your first drawings, & I have your picture also & if dear Mamma can send me the one she has of Mary Loo I will have them both fixed in one frame or Box such as I have your dear Mamma's.

During the second part of 1850 there was a double upheaval in the Prinsep household. In the earlier part of the year, GF Watts, already a habitué of 9 Chesterfield Street in the combined role of revered genius and tame family portraitist, had a breakdown in health. Sara Prinsep, whose determination to organise and smother with kindness everyone of whom she approved was equalled only by that of her sister Julia Cameron, took him in hand: he must consult the doctor at Malvern, where the Prinseps and Virginia Pattle were staying at the time. She and Virginia drove over to Eastnor Castle, where he was visiting his friend Lord Eastnor, and carried him off. Whether or not in consequence of this excursion, certainly not long afterwards, Virginia who had hitherto resisted the advances of all suitors ('everyone was in love with her,' it was said), decided to accept Lord Eastnor, soon to become the 3rd Earl Somers. They were married in October, and Virginia went off to live in a vast neo-Gothic castle in Herefordshire. She was perhaps the closest to Mia of her younger sisters, and certainly the aunt who, after Sara Prinsep, had had the most to do with the Jackson children, and her

43

engagement and marriage may well have thrown Mia's plans into confusion. In May the Jacksons were all at Leamington. By the early summer Adeline at least was staying with the Camerons at East Sheen; she and the Camerons' daughter were much of an age and may well have shared lessons. In August and September Dr Jackson was expecting his family to winter at Bonn, but in fact the three children seem to have been packed off to Spa, Mia following later, presumably after Virginia's wedding.

The second upheaval was the Prinseps' decision to leave Mayfair for Kensington. Virginia's marriage left Sara Prinsep's hands free. She had done her duty triumphantly by the two younger sisters whom she had taken on in 1845. Both were now admirably settled, Virginia married to a prospective Earl (the only Pattle husband not connected with India), Sophie to a prospective baronet. There had been good reason to stay in the centre of London while they needed to be 'taken about' (as people said) even if Thoby Prinsep's unsuccessful attempts to become a Conservative Member of Parliament had not pointed in the same direction. Now that he had abandoned thoughts of Parliament and settled for a place on the East India Company's Board of Directors, and the two girls were married, a different mode of life might be considered. When GF Watts suggested that he and the Prinseps should jointly take the lease of Little Holland House in the peaceful suburban village of Kensington, there was nothing against it. The Chesterfield Street house was given up and at the beginning of 1851 the Prinseps and Watts moved to Kensington, providing a new backcloth for the lives of their friends and relations that was to last for more than twenty years.

Meanwhile, during the summer, Sophie Dalrymple in Calcutta had had a new baby, a daughter as flourishing as her son was weakly. She was still planning to go to England at the end of the year.

Calcutta Sept 9 1850.
...Yesterday your Aunt Sophy had her little Girl christened. It is called after your aunt Virginia and a version of your Uncle John's: Julian... Virginia Julian Dalrymple is a very pretty child, very fair, like your Uncle John and has blue Eyes. It is always smiling, scarcely known to

44

cry, and I am sure your dear Mamma will be very fond of it. I was God Papa, & I gave it as my little Present - a little Silver Plate - with a Spoon and Fork.

Your next letter will be from Bonn and I shall learn how you got over the Journey, & whether it occasioned much fatigue to darling Mamma. I must close for the Post so Goodbye - God bless you my dear Child. Kiss Mary Loo & little Julia & tell them they shall have a letter next month.

*   *   *

Calcutta, Oct 3 1850

Thank you for the letter which you wrote to me from Spa, which darling Mamma enclosed in one from herself - long before this, I hope that she has rejoined you and that you are comfortably housed and have procured nice accommodations for the Winter... I suppose this will find you at Brussels, & I think that the Town will suit dear Mamma and all of you much better than your continuing at Spa during the cold weather. You will have the opportunity of carrying on your Music and Drawing lessons under good Masters, & I feel quite sure dear Addy that by the time I come home you will have some very pretty sketches ready for me to see, and will be able to play the Piano, so as to please your dear Mamma, and myself also as I am very fond of Music, & perhaps I shall think your voice like your dear Mamma's which I have always preferred to any other's. You will be amused when I tell you that your Uncle John [Dalrymple] is taking up lessons in dancing and that he goes to his dancing class twice a week. He is very well and so is Aunty Sophy she is busy making preparations for her voyage...

*   *   *

[Oct (? in error for Nov) 7 1850]

You have sent me a very interesting account of your little Journey, & the places you have visited, & given me a very nice description of some of them. There will be many objects for you to observe, and it will be better for you to note down some of them carefully so that you will be able to recollect & describe them, rather than take a hurried glance at many so as to have no clear conception of anything in particular. I have

45

Mia Jackson

no doubt that your fondness for drawing will enable you to observe the objects with much greater attention and give you a taste for that which is beautiful. I should have very much liked to be with you on your visit to Antwerp & Cologne. Perhaps when I return we may make a little tour of this kind, & then you will be able to point out to me the several objects which attracted your attention on your first visit and will have further pleasure in renewing your acquaintance with them Mamma writes cheerfully, and seems to like the air and the waters of Spa, so that I hope she will have derived a great deal of benefit from them before she is obliged to leave. I am very lonely without her, and without you all, but when I hear of you all being well, and that all the Children and you in particular are such sources of happiness to your Mamma I feel thankful that you are all spared the heat & discomfort of India, & are able to enjoy yourselves in the happy way that you are doing. Your Aunt Sophie is very busy preparing to go to England, she is to leave the 11th of December in the ship 'Nile' & will be in England the first week of April. Where will you be then.

*   *   *

Calcutta Dec 8 1850

Your Friend Miss Metcalfe arrived by the Steamer, and is staying with your Aunt Louisa [Bayley]. She came and dined with me last Evening, and gave me a long account of you and your little Sisters. She told me of the walks which you used to take together and that you had grown nearly as tall as herself, and that you were all very well when she left Spa. It is always a great pleasure to me, to meet with people who have seen you, and who are able to give me an account of you. I have received your letter by the Steamer in which you mention the arrival of your dear Mamma and that she had brought you a Daguerrotype of herself as a Present, she has sent me one and I think it very like and of course very beautiful. I hope you will be able to have nice rooms at Brussels & that you will remain there during the winter and that you will return to Spa again next Summer so that dear Mamma may have the full benefit of the waters. Your Aunty Sophy will go on board ship the day after tomorrow & your Uncle John accompanies her to Madras. Aunty Loo [Bayley] also will go down to the Sandheads with her, most likely, as her little Boy has been a little unwell. In the ship in which your

Aunty Sophy goes to England there will be 48 children. This will make a very large Nursery, & they will require a great deal of management to keep them in order.

*   *   *

[Jan 7 1851]

I have been very much entertained with the account you have sent me of the way in which you passed your Birthday, you seem to have had plenty of Fun, & the word you chose 'Innocence' was admirable for a charade & more difficult to guess than 'Looking Glass'. I can well remember & perhaps you may also the time when you used to dress yourself in my Coat and Waistcoat and Boots and come in to make your dear Mamma & myself have a hearty laugh. Your dear Mamma will recollect it very well. Charades are now very fashionable, & your Uncle [Dalrymple] who has just come from Madras where he has been with your Aunt Sophy tells me that he was at Government House at Madras, and that Sir Henry Pottinger enjoyed a Charade and took as much pleasure in it as any of the Children, or young People. Something unusual for a Governor to be playing Games of this Kind don't you think?… I hope you received the little note which I sent you last month from Miss Metcalfe. I have sent you this month a small worked Pocket handkerchief which I hope will reach you safely. It comes from Manilla and is made of the Fibre of the Pine Apple Leaf.

Early in 1851 Mia and Adeline were back in England to await the arrival of Sophie Dalrymple and her children, apparently leaving the two younger girls at Spa. Spa was clearly a success; they were to return for the summer with Mia's sisters and their children. As well as its other amenities, it provided music and drawing teachers so that these staples of the little Jacksons' education were not neglected. Other elements were sporadically introduced when Mia and Adeline were with the Prinseps at Little Holland House. The itinerant tutor Mr Phillips, who appears from time to time in Dr Jackson's letters, was probably Sara Prinsep's protégé, found for her own daughter, for he reappears in the next generation, trying with limited success to manage a Prinsep granddaughter.[3]

Calcutta March 7 1851

I have received your long and very interesting account of your visit to the Museum, and the lecture which Mr Phillips gave, and I can well imagine the delight with which you would listen to him, and endeavour to understand the Movement of the Earth and the Sun and Moon, which without the help of a good orrery and a clever Instructor is very difficult to comprehend. How greatly all knowledge adds to Happiness and to Interest in the things around one, and I am quite sure that what you have seen in the Museum and heard from Mr Phillips will make you take much more pleasure and interest in these things than you were accustomed to do before... I daresay little Julia talked a great deal about all she saw. Your dear Mamma writes me that the Winter has been very mild & that the Trees are almost coming into Bud. I hope you may have a clear and pleasant spring and that you may all be able to enjoy yourselves, and make a little tour to one of the German watering places, which would be of much service to Mamma & I hope enable her to walk about again. I should like very much to come and take a peep at you and if you remain abroad next year I must try to do so. We shall have steamers from Calcutta twice a month, and from Alexandria to Trieste there will be steamers and from Trieste to Vienna there is a carriage conveyance, and there is a railway quite thro' Austria and Germany to whatever place you may be fixed in. It would be very delightful for us all to make an Excursion together. It is three long years today, since dear Mamma went away from India and the time is very long so that I do not like to think much about it, but rather to look forward to the happy days in prospect when I may come and join you all and be a participator in your pleasures. My greatest happiness now is to have such nice accounts of you all, and to know that you are all such good and dear Children.

*   *   *

Calcutta 7 April 1851

I have received from darling Mamma your Measure and that of the other Children and I have had it all marked on the Wall. Mrs Ellerton is not so tall as you by two inches being only 5 feet high, which is very diminutive however your dear Mamma will tell you that her figure is very straight, and altho' she is now 79 years of Age she has no stoop

49

but walks very erect and tho' she has a very old face, she has a very young figure. Your dear Aunt Sarah [Prinsep] has written me a very nice account of you all, and she tells me you are grown very like your dear Mamma. I hope you will be like her in all things. You will have nowhere such a bright example. Darling Mamma appears not to have been well, and I am in hopes that she will pass a short time with Aunty Sarah and see dear Sophie and Virginia and then go to Spa for the Summer, and the German Baths, and be able to make a little journey which will do her more good than remaining so long always in one place. When I come home we must make a little tour thro' England and Scotland & perhaps visit Holland and Germany where you will have many things to shew me. Your Mamma tells me that you are making a very pretty sketch of an Archway. Never leave any of your time unoccupied, and every day before you go to bed think over what you have done and learned during the day, and it would do you good also to make a memorandum of it. Whilst you are enjoying the pleasant spring and taking your morning walk in the Fields, I am either busy in driving along the dusty hot roads of Calcutta or sitting underneath the Punkah at home to keep cool, but I never think of this, or give way to any mourning when I receive cheerful accounts of you all and learn that you are doing all you can to improve your minds and to be a comfort to darling Mamma.

*   *   *

[May 1851]
I have received your letter telling me that the Handkerchief had reached you and that you were pleased with it. I have also heard from you after you had seen your Aunty Sophy in London. This will reach you most likely at Spa where I hope you will all be passing the Summer and Autumn & be gaining health and strength and that the place will suit darling Mamma and enable her to walk about. Your Aunty Sophy had written me and told me how happy she was to see you looking so well and such a comfort to dear Mamma. This I am quite sure you will always be. When you get back to Spa, you will have to make up for this long holiday and set to work at your Music and drawing with double vigour. I shall expect some of your little sketches. I have sent you a Book by a Gentleman who will call upon your Mamma in Spa, and who

will give you an account of me as he has been passing the last three months with me. I am sure that you have enjoyed your visit to Aunty Sophy and be glad after it is over to return to your sisters at Spa. How happy they will be to see you also. I have sent a little Book to Julia & you must get her to read some of the little tales to you.

*   *   *

[July 3 1851]

I have received a nice account of your visit to the Exhibition and have been very much interested in it, the Enjoyment you experienced I can well imagine, & if darling Mamma could but have accompanied you, the delight would have been perfect.[4] I have seen the Illustrated London News, and I can imagine how great and overpowering the whole scene must have appeared to you. I think you have shewn your Taste in admiring the Sculpture of the Greek slave. Generally speaking there is always something more chaste and impressive in beautiful sculpture than in painting and one of these days I hope I may have the pleasure of taking you to see some of Roubilliac's sculpture in Westminster Abbey and at one of the colleges in Cambridge. It is very sad to learn that dear Mamma continues so weak. You must try to get her Well and cheer her spirits and I hope that the residence at Spa and the Happiness of having your Aunts with her and their children will keep her from drooping, during the next four months and that you may have the winter in England. I wish I could come and join you at the Fireside and be able to go out with you on your walks. We have the rains at present and I scarcely ever walk out but am in my carriage the greater part of the day, so that I shall have to learn again almost to walk and have no doubt I shall very soon be tired. Now that you have your Aunts with you and so many cousins you must take care dear Addy that you do not get disposed to lay aside your habits of application for the pleasure of having a Chat with them. I shall hope to receive some nice sketches from you, and to learn that you have got on well with your Music. I am very fond of Music as your Mamma will tell you.

*   *   *

Calcutta 5th Augt [1851]

Thank you for your amusing little description of your visit to the Waterfall. It was very kind of Mr Bayley[5] to accompany you, but I have no doubt that he enjoyed it as much as you all did, & he wrote that he had been very much pleased with the visit and gave me a very nice account... We have no cascades in Bengal nothing but one continuous plain, which would be wearying for the Eye to rest on, if it were not for the beauty of the foliage, the beautifully mixed green of the Trees and the different shades which these reflect when lighted up by the Sunshine in an Indian Sky. I am glad to find you are fond of natural effects, for they are always improving to the Mind, and their varied Character is but a proof of the great Omniscient Mind which conceived and made them. How superior is the beautiful structure of a simple Leaf to all the wonderful works of art which are collected in the Great Museums. But I shall be giving a lecture rather than a letter and so my dear Child I must end and will only tell you how much I long for your cheerful presence and that of your dear Mamma and your sisters, and how happy I shall feel when I have you all around me again. It is this prospect that helps me on in my daily work and cheers me for the many hours that I am journeying about in my Carriage.

Sometime before the middle of 1851 it must have been decided that Mia should not return to India at all, but should find a house near London where she and the children might await Dr Jackson's return. While Mia's health was the obvious and central reason for this decision, there may also have been a real problem about the children. Many Anglo-Indian families had two sets of relations to share the responsibility for children deposited in England, and often a supply of willing maiden aunts. The Bayleys and Dalrymples seem to have had no difficulty in making arrangements for their young. But even if there were Jacksons nearer than Lincolnshire, it seems unlikely that either parent would have considered them suitable; they belonged to a different world and had effectively vanished from the scene.[6] At the other end of the social scale, the newly married Eastnors could hardly be expected to absorb Virginia's three nieces, and while both the Camerons and the Prinseps would undoubtedly have stood by, perhaps dividing the children between them, how much simpler if Mia stayed at home and brought up her daughters herself! Whatever the balance of ingredients in the decision, it was taken, and everyone settled down to a still longer separation. Mia found a suitable house at 9 Well Walk, Hampstead, and there they remained. From that point her health steadily improved.

[Sept 1851]

I did not receive any letter from you by the last mail. You were away from your dear Mamma at Spa, and perhaps this was the cause. I shall be very happy when I hear that you are all fixed in a House of your own where you can remain until I come home to see you. I hope you will get some pretty place, not too far from London, and that you will have a nice Garden of flowers, & have plenty of Blackbirds & Thrushes to build their nests, and come out and sing in the morning. I have been to see the Victoria Regia[7] at the Botanical Garden here, the flower is not so large as the one you wrote about, but I daresay it will be, or that others will spring up of the same size. It is very pretty, and I should have enjoyed the visit which I paid to it very much if I had not been in constant fear of the boat being upset, and I had no desire to get a dipping in one of the deep Pools at the Botanical Gardens... It added very much to my pleasure in seeing it, because I knew that you had been to see the one at Kensington. The flowers in India are all very large and beautiful but they are for the most part without scent, we have no Violets or Primroses. But in the large forests of India there are Trees the size of Oaks covered with fine red flowers, some with orange coloured flowers, & you can well conceive their beauty when the sun comes out upon them...

Your Aunt Louisa [Bayley] has now gone to Midnapore, she writes to me very often and tells me that her two little Boys are quite well. She sent me your letter to read & I was very much pleased with it.

*   *   *

[Oct 8 1851]

I was very glad indeed to receive your letter which was the only one that I received from the Children. I suppose Mary Loo and Julia were tired, & that it was a greater effort for them to write than for you. Your dear

Mamma told me that she was better, and able to move about a little, & to feel quite Independent in the House. This was very good news for me, and I feel very thankful for it and I hope that during next spring she will quite regain her Health. Your Aunt Louisa [Bayley] is now at Midnapore, her little Boys have both been ill and little William suffering from Fever, I am very sorry that they have left Calcutta they are now near 100 Miles off, and as we have no railroad in India the distance is very far. In England you would think nothing of it. We are all very glad to learn that dear little Hewy [Dalrymple] is so much Better and that Brighton has suited him so well. Your Uncle John has been made quite happy by the last accounts By the Steamer which leaves today a Lady Mrs Elliott[8] is going to England, & she said that she should like very much to see you and your sisters and I have given her the Direction and if you are in Town when she arrives I hope darling Mamma will send you, she will tell you about me. Give my love to Aunty Sophy & tell her that her John is very well - that he often comes to see me...

* * *

[Nov 7 1851]

The arrival of the Steamer always gives me very great pleasure, as I then look for letters from my dear Children. By the last mail I received a long and very interesting letter from you, and one from Mary and little Julia. I am quite lighthearted again in hearing that dear Mamma is better and able to move about, with much care during the present Season I hope that she will be able next year, to be still more independent and to go with you to the several Places of Interest in which London abounds, as well as to take a walk of one or two Miles. I shall then feel that she is really pretty well... Mamma tells me that you are going to visit dear Aunt Virginia at Eastnor. It will be a pleasant visit and I think you will enjoy the little stay there very much. But you may enjoy the sight of all these things without having any desire to possess them; and the little quiet house where dear Mamma is, will be more than everything else to you. There are few things that more conduce to happiness than an unselfish mind.

I must not forget to tell you that your Uncle John has received dear Sophy's picture and been very much delighted with it, but I do not like

it as much as the side face which I have of dear Mamma & yourself.
This is the best of Mr Watts's likenesses…

References

1. Mrs. Marcet, 1769-1858, was the much-read author of *Conversations on Chemistry, especially for the Female Sex* (1806), and similar works.
2. The Governor-General was returning to the capital after the annexation of the Punjab.
3. L. Troubridge. *Memories and Recollections*. London, 1925, p.50
4. The Great Exhibition in Hyde Park, 1851.
5. Was this Uncle Henry? The Bayleys were a large Bengal clan and it may have been another member of the family.
6. The elder Mrs. Jackson seems to have lived in London (first Bloomsbury, then Notting Hill) for some time before her death in 1858, perhaps with a married daughter or with one of the relations with whom Mrs. Ellerton corresponded. It seems unlikely that she and the Little Holland House ladies saw much of each other, though no doubt the proprieties were observed.
7. A large South American water lily, recently introduced both to Europe, where it was flowered at Chatsworth in 1849 by Joseph Paxton, and to India. Adeline would have seen it at the Great Exhibition.
8. Mrs. Elliott was a friend of Mrs. Ellerton's.

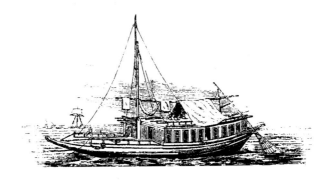

Hooghli boat of the type that capsized with the Archdeacon

55

(iii) 1852

At the beginning of 1852 Dr Jackson was still reckoning on getting to England sometime the following year. The earlier plan, when Mia was expected to come back for a few years in India, seems to have been that he would then retire for good. 'We shall have no more separations,' he had written. But he was now thinking rather of drawing on his unused entitlement to European furlough, spending some months with his family and then returning to Calcutta for a final stint. With the expenses of Mia's illness (and the frequent changes of scene that were then thought the right thing for almost every complaint) and now the Hampstead household to maintain, there were obvious attractions in another year or two of putting money by before settling down to a new pattern of life in England. Besides, he was interested in his work in India. 1853 would be a good time for a break, for the grand new Medical College Hospital would just have come into use, presumably with a major reorganisation of medical posts and with a general feeling in the Calcutta medical world that one stage of its work had been completed and another begun.

John Dalrymple had moved to other quarters when Sophie and the children had left for England at the end of 1850 and there had been a year without in-laws at the Jackson house. Now another of Mia's sisters, Louisa Bayley, was in residence, though only temporarily. Mrs Ellerton was inclined to think Louisa 'pleasure-loving,' but had nothing but good to say of Henry Bayley; she was later to declare in the course of a gossip about Pattle husbands that she would rather take him with five hundred rupees a month than John Dalrymple with five thousand. He was also a close friend of her nephew. There were thus none of the difficult undercurrents to life in the household that there had been two years before.

[Jan 7 1852]
Thank you for your nice letter written to me on my Birthday... This time next year under God's Blessing I may be making preparations for joining you, & sharing in all your little joys and pleasures. I am afraid

to think too much about it, I have another hot season to get through & another rains to get over,. The time passes very quickly, for your dear Mamma will tell you that I am not a very idle Person - but am very exact and punctual - very regular in my hours of sitting down to Breakfast at 9 o'clock & at Dinner & so forth. Generally in India People do not know the value of time, & regularity, we have no railways, & the people in India never say that they will do any thing today but always - Kul Kurega - I will do it tomorrow which tomorrow often never comes. These habits have extended to the English also. I suppose in dear Mamma's house you will have everything very punctual and in this way no one is ever kept waiting. There is nothing I dislike so much as irregularity... Your Aunt Louisa with their two little Boys are staying with me at present, and I expect your Uncle Henry [Bayley] next week.

*   *   *

[Feb 8 1852]

The Daguerrotypes of you and your sister arrived by the last Steamer and they are very beautiful and are great treasures. I have been delighted with them and everyone who has seen them has been pleased with them. The comparison with the one I had of you some years ago shews how much you have grown, and gives much more of thoughtful expression than appeared in the old one... I shall now quite know your face if I were to meet you anywhere. I am very glad that you like Hampstead so much and that you have got so nice a House and Garden, with the advantage of plenty of Water. We shall all have a Happy Home together when I come and join you, & the thought of this will keep me up during the present hot season. If you like the place now that it is Winter the Spring and Summer will open fresh beauties to you and make you like the place better still, and I think that it will suit darling Mamma & that she may at last find a spot where she is able to get strength and health. Clear air and Mountain or Hilly scenery suits her better than the plains and I hear that Malvern suited her better than any spot she has visited. When I come you will be able to shew me all the beauties of Hampstead. Your Aunt Louisa [Bayley] has been staying with me the last two months whilst Uncle Henry has been moving to his new station and whilst the house is undergoing repairs... I had a very pretty pocket Book which little Addy and Mia [Bayley] sent me out by the last Mail if I am not able to write will you let them know that it is a very useful present.

*   *   *

7 Feb [? March intended] 1852
... I am going tomorrow to the Botanical Gardens for a visit. Your Aunt Louisa went there yesterday to see a Wild Bull taken by a Spanish Gentleman who was skilled in throwing the Lasso, which is a long rope with a noose at the end, in which they catch the Bull by the Legs, or by the Head and throw him down. It so happened however yesterday that there was no Wild Bull, but a number of timid Cows, which ran away when the Spaniard went near them to throw the rope over one so that your Aunty Loo had no opportunity of seeing the Wild Bull tamed. The Gentleman then threw the noose of the rope over the top of a Palm Tree to shew the Ladies how it was done, to the great distress of the Botanist Dr Falconer who has as much affection for his Palm Trees as many Fathers have for their Children. So Aunty Loo had the journey for nothing.

*   *   *

Calcutta April 7 1852
I have always very great pleasure in receiving your monthly letter and reading the long accounts which you give of your dear Sisters and Mamma. The letters from Home always cheer me out [sic], & make the time pass quickly between each Mail. It is a source of great comfort to me to find that you are all keeping so well, & that darling Mamma has improved so greatly as to be able to move about, and really to be gaining strength, I know how trying the hot weather used to be here, that I shall still feel a little anxious until I hear how she gets through the English Summer.
Hampstead appears to have been quite the place of all others for you... I am sending by the present Mail some Indian seeds which I am sure you and your sisters will take great pleasure in tending and I hope that they may live and bring forth flowers, & if they should succeed I am quite sure you will take the greater pleasure in them because your Papa has sent them...

I have written to dear Mamma about a Piano & I hope she will be able to procure a good one for the pleasure of playing is always increased when the Instrument is good - still this requires practice as every thing else does to be done well - for there is no royal rail road to knowledge. It is only to be gained by labour and Attention and when things are well learnt & thought over in youth they are never forgotten.

It is a safe guess that by 1852 Little Holland House was already established as the place remembered with such affection, and some amusement, by Victorian writers of reminiscences; Sara Prinsep was not nicknamed 'Dash' for nothing. The old family friendship with Thackeray (who seems to have fallen under the charm of at least two of the Pattle sisters when they were girls) and the new friendship with Watts had provided her with a ready-made circle of painters and poets and clever young men prepared to be interested in painting and poetry. Thoby Prinsep and the Camerons brought in figures from politics and learning, and if Mrs Prinsep perceived a gap she took her own measures to fill it. It is said that when she wished to make the acquaintance of the Oxford Professor of History, HH Vaughan, who had a great reputation for brilliance amongst his contemporaries, she simply drove up to the Athenaeum Club and carried him off to Kensington in her carriage. Whether this capture was the cause of the visit to Oxford reported by Adeline to her father, or perhaps its consequence, Vaughan was thenceforward one of the Little Holland House habitués, and enveloped by the Pattle ladies' adulation. Quietly as Mia lived, she had her share of the Prinseps' world and clearly liked her daughters to profit by the opportunities on offer. There were always a good many children eating strawberries or playing on the swings at Little Holland House during those summer Sunday afternoons, when the drawing room furniture was brought into the garden and Rossetti, Burne Jones, Thackeray, Tennyson and Carlyle strolled under the trees, and it could not be denied that it was all a good deal more amusing than Calcutta. Perhaps Dr Jackson occasionally found it uphill work to respond adequately to his eldest daughter's widening interests, and if his letters harp to what may seem an excessive degree on hard work, thoroughness, and so on, he may have felt that some counterweight to the Pattle ladies' successive cultural enthusiasms would not come amiss.

In the spring of 1852, Lord Dalhousie, having dealt with the Punjab and shaken up his central administration, turned his attention to Burma, where there had been worse trouble than usual between British merchants and the Burmese. There was the usual sequence of fruitless diplomatic notes and warnings, and at the beginning of April the Bengal army was sent in to round off the annexations of twenty-five years before. Once more all thoughts of release from medical duty were at an end. Dr Jackson, like his colleagues, was pinned down in Calcutta; and, since there was a limit to the number of surgeons permitted to be absent simultaneously, all plans for future furlough were in suspense.

[3 May 1852]
I have again been disappointed in procuring some Indian seeds to send you in my Packet, and I am almost afraid that the summer will have passed before they can reach you. Seeds in England do not spring up so quickly as they do here, for in Bengal one or two months generally brings up the seed, & a Shrubbery of large plants will be made in a couple of years, whilst in England many years are required to get anything like a decent Shrubbery. Every thing in the vegetable world is on the grand scale. The Plantain with their long broad leaves, the thick foliage of every common Tree would form an excellent hiding place for anyone who wished to use it as such. I long however for the sight of a Primrose which I have not seen these 22 years, & the sweet scent of a violet bed would be more grateful than the gaudy flowers and the deep green foliage of our finest trees. And now just when I hoped to have in prospect a Journey to you all and to be made happy by seeing your dear cheerful faces, something unexpected comes to prevent it. Only think that because there is War between India & Burmah, that a Papa is not allowed to go home & see his Children. Perhaps it may be over next year but this is quite uncertain, & in the meantime we must live in Hope.

How do you like the new Piano? Has Mamma been able to procure one of good tone for you & do you still continue to like your Music lessons? & get on with the German Master... By the present Mail I have sent you a square Shawl of Cashmere it is Scarlet with a deep border and I hope

The Marquis of Dalhousie, Governor General, 1848-56

61

that darling Mamma will not dislike it. I intended to have sent something of a different kind for you & for your sisters but the Parcel has not reached Calcutta & perhaps may have to wait another two mails for it. So you must tell dear Mary & Little Julia that dear Papa has not forgotten them.

*   *   *

Calcutta July 2 1852

I have been very much pleased by your long and interesting letter giving me an account of your visit to Oxford, and your attendance when Mr Vaughan lectured. Both the subjects were matters of much Interest. The landing of the Danes & their stay in England is one especially so, and in the country where I have passed most of my young days, namely Lincolnshire, there are the remains of their residence marked by peculiarity of names of villages similar to those which occur in Denmark and all along the Sea Coast this is more especially observed… I hope you may have been able to have been at other lectures of Dr Vaughan & perhaps your dear Mamma will have taken you. It is a great distance for you to have gone & some expense also. The Seeds which I have sent for your garden will reach you rather late in the Year & perhaps prove unproductive. We have no bulbs here that I could send & are dependant on the Cape of Good Hope chiefly for them... The flower most prized here is the Violet & I have never seen a Primrose or Cowslip since I have been in India.

This must be a very short letter for I have to write a great many & have very little time.

*   *   *

Calcutta 5 Aug 1852

I did not write by the last steamer, as your dear Mamma will tell you, because I had no time; since then, I have received a long letter from you at East Sheen; and I have also received the pair of Slippers which you had worked for me; They are very pretty, and as soon as Mrs Ellerton is sufficiently recovered to fill up the unfinished leaf I will send them to the China man, & will have a pair of comfortable Slippers made, which I shall daily wear, & I hope bring home with me to England. I wanted a pair of Slippers, and these have come most opportunely. I

62

have received your composition on the Seasons & have been very much pleased with it. The Seasons you will observe vary altogether as you are either in the Northern or Southern hemisphere... In India where there is a great deal of Sun, and abundance of rain, the Grass grows most rapidly and the Trees are so covered with leaves that many native villages are quite concealed by the luxuriance of the Foliage. We have no little Robins here and no singing birds to make our walks cheerful, and we have very few nicely scented flowers.

I shall hope to receive a full description of Bonn and the Rhine & Drakenfels and all the pretty places that you visit. I hope you will keep a Journal. It will be a great amusement to you in looking over it when you return to England, and you must keep it to shew me, when I come home & have you all around me, at some quiet pretty Cottage.

*   *   *

Calcutta Sep 7 1852

I am glad to find that the Shawl arrived safely & that you are pleased with it. I hope that the Cashmere cloth has also been received & that your Mamma had been able to make you some warm Cloaks etc. for the weather does not I fancy now allow of your complaint that it is too hot. I was very sad to find that you were all so drooping when the last letters reached...

Your Aunt Louisa is very busy making preparations for her voyage in the Steamer called the Queen of the South. I am sending by the same ship a Box containing the Picture of your Aunts Virginia & Sophie when they were little girls & I am sending a Picture of Aunt Ellerton which is for my Mother.[1] I am not going to have any further attempts to have either a picture or a daguerrotype taken in Calcutta as my former attempts were so unsuccessful. Everyone that sees your Daguerrotypes & your Sisters is pleased with them and anxious to know the Artist. Your Mamma tells me of your visit to the Picture Gallery and to the Colosseum all these sights are interesting & instructive, perhaps we may one of these days be able to pay a visit to the Louvre & see the grand Picture of the late Marshall Soult by Murillo it seems to be the grandest of its kind. There are some fine paintings in the Fitzwilliam Museum at Cambridge which I shall like to shew. One of the Virgin and the Child by Carlo Dolci. I hope you are making progress with your drawing & Music & singing. I have written to dear Mamma especially to say that I wish you to have Masters for Music for I know dear Child that you will make the most of the Instruction & that it will be a great source of Happiness and pleasure in after years.

*   *   *

At this point there is an unexpected sighting of Dr Jackson against a professional rather than a domestic background. Some six years earlier, a Dr Balaguer had turned up in Calcutta seeking government employment on the strength of his method of treating cholera (and a wide variety of other diseases) by the use of the 'medicated hot air bath' that he claimed to have invented. The Bengal Medical Board had advised him to apply to the Medical College Hospital for permission to demonstrate the efficacy of his treatment, and he had been given every facility to do so between April and June 1846. No appointment had followed. He had now tried again, from London this time, by direct application to the East India Company, citing a list of successes and adding a collection of references, one from Dr Jackson, who had been in clinical charge of the hospital at the time of his demonstration. The papers were sent from London to Calcutta, the Medical Board sent them to the Secretary of the Medical College, still Dr Mouat and now Professor of Medicine as well as Secretary, and Dr Mouat very properly sent them on to Dr Jackson. Here was one of those many letters to which he had to devote the hot middle hours of the day, and he dealt with it promptly.

Promptly, but not altogether easily. Dr Balaguer's treatment had consisted in removing the patient from his bed to sit in a large tin tub where he was exposed to the hot air, medicated with ingredients and delivered by methods that the inventor did not reveal either at the time or when he left. 'He carried his secret with him,' Dr Jackson noted. This secrecy had been very ill-received at the time and continued to rankle. Still, Dr Jackson was anxious to be fair. He had found the treatment valuable in the early stages of cholera, as also in certain cases of

Dr Frederick Mouat, bust by W.H. Thorneycroft, 1847

65

rheumatism and dropsy, and had no hesitation in saying so. In the later stages, however, 'it failed like other remedies to do good.' He had indeed at times been obliged 'to remove the Patient from the position lest he should die in the bath.' As to Dr Balaguer's list of successes, he noted that the cholera epidemic in 1846 had been mild, with more recoveries than usual. If, as he understood, Dr Balaguer had now revealed the components of the medication he had used, he 'would not desire to withhold from him the merit which he undoubtedly possesses of introducing so valuable an adjunct in the treatment of this disease.' But it was useful only as an adjunct and then only at the beginning of an attack. Having delivered himself of this opinion, he sent the bundle of papers back to Dr Mouat.

Dr Mouat was much more trenchant. He did not want Dr Balaguer anywhere near his hospital, and with the records under his hand he set out the case against him in some detail. The tub had been very inconvenient and awkward to handle, the treatment was not new - it had been tried in Russia and at Stettin - and it achieved nothing that could not be done better by mustard plaster, ginger friction or hot water bottles. It was also cruel: the European patients had threatened to smash the apparatus if it were gone on with. Finally he produced the figures showing the cholera mortality rates for both European and Indian patients in April and May of the five years that included Dr Balaguer's sojourn at the hospital from which it was apparent that his experiments had altered nothing. No more was heard of Dr Balaguer, and his primitive form of sauna passed (like mesmerism) into oblivion.

The letters to Adeline resume.

Calcutta Oct 4th 1852

Thank you for the letter which has come by the Steamer, it has given me very great pleasure as indeed all your letters do, and I am very glad to find that you are all so well, and that you are making progress in your studies. I have received the Maps and the drawings and have been very much pleased and amused with them. The former were I suppose drawn from Memory... I hope you [are] drawing also and shall be glad to hear that your Mamma has been able to get you a good drawing

66

Master who will make you thoroughly acquainted with the Principles of the Art, so that you may be able to teach your younger sisters, who will all look up to you for instruction; and you will also go on with your Music. I know that there is a great deal to do but with strong determination to excel in all that you undertake, I am quite sure dear Addy you will succeed. There is also another little branch of Study which young Ladies do not know much about, & do not think it necessary to attend to, and that is Arithmetic. I shall want you to be able to keep my accounts when I come home and shall expect to find you acquainted with all the rules in common use, & I have no doubt you will be. I hope that you continue to use the Piano, & that the Music Teacher answers well. Nothing dear Addy is to be learned without labour and application; and the brightest and most learned among all Classes are those who have fagged the hardest. Never mind therefore the time it takes to do a thing - only be determined to do it well - for if it is worth your while to do anything, it is worth your while to do it well. I shall be very glad to have your map of Greece.

*   *   *

Nov 7 1852 Calcutta

This day week will be your Birthday when you will be 15 years of age. I shall think of you when the day comes & offer up my Prayers that you may in all things be like your dear darling Mamma, & shall give you my blessing in Spirit. I have enclosed my normal little token of Remembrance, & shall beg of you to bestow it as most agreeable to yourself and I hope you will all be happy and merry when Christmas comes. I have sent a Box containing several little presents. There is a small Bombay Box for you & one for little Alice [Prinsep] which you must give her with my love & there are two other little Boxes one for Mary and one for Julia. By this time you will have your Aunt Louisa home and her little Children. What a large party of Cousins there will be and Hampstead will form quite a little Colony for you all. I have sent to dear Mamma a very useful Atlas which you will find of great Interest. It gives a very good sketch of the Heavenly Bodies explaining their Motion; & gives a variety of Maps explanatory of the different races of Man, Animals & plants who inhabit the Earth and then a Geographical description of each Country. I expect that it will afford you much Interest. I am glad to find that you have read the History of the Danes... In India we are well supplied with new Books every month by the Steamer, & many of the best works published are in distribution within a few weeks of their first appearance in London. I belong to a Book Club. A young Lady is the Secretary who sends round the Books marking up the number of days that are allowed for the reading & sending for them when the day arrives. We have no circulating Libraries & are obliged either to adopt this plan or to purchase each Book for ourselves & in Calcutta this is expensive.

*　　　*　　　*

Calcutta Dec 10 1852

...Today I have been to breakfast with the Bishop of Calcutta to meet the Bishop of Victoria from China. I took Mrs Ellerton with me: a large party of 30 assembled & as each arrived the Bishop of Calcutta met them and had some conversation. Then we all went into a long room arranged as a Chapel. One of the clergy read a portion of the Psalms & the Bishop expounded, another portion was read, and another Exposition until the whole Psalm had been gone through. Then the Bishop offered up a prayer more especially with reference to the Churches & Schools of China. I have been however sometimes there when the Bishop has offered up a prayer for dear Mamma's restoration to health, especially when she first went home. When Prayers were ended we went into Breakfast. I took in to Breakfast[2] a young lady about 16 who had just arrived from England & to whom everything was new she would have liked to remain in Calcutta but was going up to the Hills with her sister who had come out with her. After Breakfast was over the Bishop of Victoria was invited to tell the friends there assembled something about China & the Missions there established & he gave a very interesting account of the Missionaries in China, and told us that the most successful of the Missionaries were those who resided in [illegible] where they all lived in the Native Town amongst the Natives and had their Morning and Evening Service to which the Natives frequently came & that the good Influence of the Missionaries was very great amongst them. The Chinese are followers of Confucius & worshippers of Boodh. They are very clever and well informed & tho' they fully admit the excellency of the Christian religion to their own they are unwilling to give up their own religion, because of their dislike to any change. I have to leave this for the Mail closes at 3 & I have barely time to write to dearest Mamma.

References

1. Dr. Jackson later gave Mrs. Ellerton much pleasure by having several copies of the lithograph made for her to give to her friends. (The Dalrymples however were "haughty and contemptuous" about it.)
2. Doctors, though part of the army, did not take rank; a Presidency Surgeon, drawing the pay of a Lieutenant Colonel, went in to a formal meal behind a subaltern. Hence, presumably, this rather odd pairing.

The new Calcutta Medical College

(iv) 1853

Sophie Dalrymple, accompanied by a French maid, was back in India early in 1853, bringing her brother-in-law news of home, more slippers (finished this time, if not yet made up) and a fresh supply of daguerreotypes; and she and her husband were added to the Jackson household until they could go off to John Dalrymple's new post in East Bengal. This visit was expected to last a fortnight and in fact lasted two months. It came just at the time when Dr Jackson had hoped to be setting out to see his wife and children and it is perhaps no wonder that when it was over he felt the need for a break and took the first proper holiday of his Indian service. A sea voyage, to Cape Town or perhaps Singapore and back, was the stock Calcutta prescription for feeling below par but he was not a good sailor and he preferred to make for Ceylon. Charles Cameron had served in the island before going to India and he had since bought land there, hoping to make a fortune from growing coffee, so that Dr Jackson would find connections when he arrived.

Calcutta Jan 5 1853

... I was very sorry to learn from darling Mamma that you had been ill, & that you were suffering from Cold & in bed when she last wrote. Some Influenza I suppose, which is so common in England the beginning of Autumn & is not infrequent in Calcutta also during the cold weather. Our season here however is very pleasant from November to February, and I think for that period it would suit you very well. How should you like a Voyage to India? to remain with your Papa during the Cold Weather. Are you very ill at Sea? You have made some little excursions across the Channel and would be able to judge... I want very much to see you all and to have you with me & I sometimes think that if I am unable to come home I shall beg darling Mamma to bring you out to see me for a Cold Weather and go back again or go to some of the Hills such as Ceylon or the Neelgherries until we can all go home together. I do hope however that I shall be able to get home.

*　　　*　　　*

70

Calcutta Feb 19 1853

I was unable to answer your last letter by the return mail owing to its departure being so close. Your Aunt Sophy arrived very well and gave me the most delightful accounts of you all. She delivered to me the maps and the drawings which were all very nicely executed, & she brought me also the slippers which you so thoughtfully had worked for me with your own hands. I have had them made up, and I wear them every day. They came to me most opportunely and when I come home I shall bring them with me. You have managed your maps very well, and the names of the places are all written with great distinctness. I was also very much pleased with the drawings but I think you might have a little improvement if you have the advantage also of another Master, but dear Mamma will settle all this. By the present steamer there is a Box of Bonbons and other little things which you will divide amongst yourselves and distribute to your Cousins, & I hope will be pleased with them. There is an Illustrated copy of the New Testament which your dear Mamma gave to you many years ago & will be the more prized now than It would at the time it first had your name written in it. Your Aunt Sophie is very well and very happy to be back again; I shall not see very much of her as she is to leave for the Mofussil in a fortnight's time and perhaps I may not then see her again before I come home. She has brought out the pictures of little Hewy and Virginia & they are very much altered from what they were when they left this, but not more I think than Aunt Sophie is herself for she has become very rosy in her complexion & is much stronger and stouter than she was when she left this. How rejoiced I shall be to find such a Change in darling Mamma. I have all your daguerrotypes, but your Aunt tells me that Little Julia has quite grown out of hers.

* * *

Calcutta April 5 1853

Colds and sore throats have been as troublesome in Calcutta as in England during the past month, altho we have neither Frost nor Snow and are endebted to America for every piece of Ice which we have to cool our Water[1] and sit under a Punkah night and day to get some cool air. I am very sorry to hear from dearest Mamma that you had been so unwell as to be confined to bed with a sore throat... Tell darling

71

Mamma that I have just had a present of Rosewater from an old Lady who lives next door who seems to know my predilection for that scent in the hot weather & generally sends me a supply. I wish I could give it to you.

Your Aunt Sophie with Uncle John & Eugenie left me yesterday for Chittagong which is a station at the Eastern Corner of the Bay of Bengal a place that your dear Mamma & I went many years ago & I daresay you have still some recollections of it. Noacally which is the place that they will ultimately go to is about 70 miles from Chittagong & they will have to journey by Palanqueens. How it will make Eugenie's fat sides shake.

I have sent you some verses on the death of the Duke of Wellington written by my friend Sir Laurence Peel. They have not the beauty of Tennyson's Rhyme but still they are not with[out] much poetical Spirit & I think they will interest you and darling Mamma. Do not destroy them but keep them.

*   *   *

Galle May 16 [1853]

A few lines from this little spot which you can scarcely remember to have visited when you came home with your darling Mamma & sister Mary will I think interest you. I have left Calcutta for a few weeks change and preferred coming to Ceylon to any other place... The harbour at Galle is confined at its entrance by high rocks and has a very pretty picturesque appearance. The Class of people are like those of Madras or Calcutta only in appearance more effeminate, so that when you see the back you can scarcely distinguish the Man from the Woman, as they all wear Tortoise shell combs in their Hair, which any fine London Lady might not be ashamed to put on her head. The upper part of the body is naked and a tight silken or cotton coloured dress is wrapped tightly around the waist. Our passengers are all busy in purchasing ornaments of different kinds, stones such as you used to get at Brighton Topazes, Sapphires etc. I would have obt^d some of the Tortoise shell bracelets for you if I had met with an opportunity of sending them home, but I did not like to ask any of the passengers to take charge. Tomorrow morning I shall start by Coach to Colombo & then pass on to Candy...

*   *   *

Galle June 4 1853

My last letter to you was from this place on my arrival in the Island, but as I have now made a tour thro' the greater part of it, I am able to tell you more about this Emerald Isle which must rival and I think excel in beauty that which has for so long a time had this designation. The Island is one piece of verdure throughout, nothing but the varied green of old and young Forest, with the different patches of Cultivation interspersed here and there. The road from Galle to Colombo a distance of 72 Miles is as picturesque a drive as you can imagine. The Sea runs upon your left hand the whole way, the Billows rising where the rocks which come close in upon the road and the beautiful spouting of the water chasing as it were each other with the white sea foam which bursts forth as it comes to the shore gives it a most entrancing appearance, in one place the Tide which was high water as we passed came over the road and in general it comes up very close. The Shore has too rocky an Aspect to allow many boats being seen and it is only where there is Sand that more are found. In many places we had to cross either by lengthened bridges of Boats, or in a Ferry, large Rivers or arms of the sea with the most beautiful appearance of inland Lakes stretching out into the land with the Trees coming down to the water's edge. Your dear Mamma will recollect something of the kind in passing through the Sunderbunds of Bengal when you were a little Girl coming down from Ghazipore, but this far surpasses it in beauty.

The whole line of the Road is covered with Cocoa Nut Trees and Palm Trees. The Natives believe that the Cocoa Nut Tree will not grow beyond the sound of human voices, they certainly thrive much better near their own dwellings and they form part of their main support for many convert the nut into Currie, drink the juice and indeed live on them, and live under them, the Cocoa Nut forms the chief part of their houses, the walls are built from the stem and the roof covered with its branches. They make their mats out of its fibres and all their fishing nets of the same, so that it contributes almost to every necessity of life and you can well imagine their affection for this Tree and enter into the feelings of the African detailed in one of Mrs Heman's beautiful little pieces which your dear Mamma will shew you if you do not already know it, when on visiting Kew Gardens the Man 'clasped his Country's Tree and wept.'

73

Every now and then we passed along the road we came upon a large Lizard about 4 feet long who was taking his stroll unconcernedly or we saw the lively green Chameleon or Lizard sporting about or running up the branches of the Trees. Amongst our fellow passengers were 3 Pigeons which the Editor of one of the Newspapers in Colombo employs to bring the Intelligence from Galle on the arrival of the steamer. They are daintily fed at Colombo and then sent down to await the arrival of the Mail, and they make the return journey backwards & forwards in the Coach & are let out of their Cage midway, by way of practise. It was interesting to see the way these intelligent creatures acted as soon as the Lid of the Basket was opened. They rose high up into the air, then made a short circuit, then... the three birds took the straight line and flew on to Colombo where they would reach in 20 minutes the distance being 32 miles.

There is nothing very striking about the people who are like other Asiatics, very effeminate particularly near Galle. The middle aged people so disfigure their mouths by eating the cocoanut the Paun and tobacco they have always a dirty appearance together with black Teeth. In the Candian or Hill province the men and women are more Athletic and have bolder countenances, but the former still adhere to the Feminine custom of wearing two Combs in their Hair, a round one on the Crown of the head and a very high straight one on the back, & you may conceive the Grotesque appearance of the Governor's servants who wear a Soldier's Coat, their own Garment of silk or Cotton wreathed round the body, & the Combs in the Hair certainly they don't look very Martial. I had not an opportunity of seeing Boodh's Tooth which is a valuable relic greatly prized by the Candians kept under 4 Covers or Cascs in the Temple at Candy. It has been made over now to their priests, the Government not having anything to do with this Relic and whilst I was in Candy a priest was selected by the Candian Government to receive charge of it. These people dress differently from the rest of the people. They have always a yellow covering over their body, & appear to have great Influence upon the People. It is amusing to see them travel about in small carriages drawn by a Bullock who trots away like a pony.

How much I should have liked for you and your dear Mamma & sisters to have been present with me to witness the several waterfalls and extensive views which every now and then broke upon my sight. The

Climate was very cool, I rode out and walked all day, & in the upper part of the province near your uncle Charles Cameron's Estate I had a fire every night and washed myself at the water which came from the rock. On my way down in coming through a very narrow path I came upon a Spider's web the strength of which was so strong that the gentleman who was with me informed me that small birds are often caught & held in them. There was a large Butterfly in this one, but as the web came against my face in riding through the defile it seemed like a piece of silk, so strong. The Insect is not quite like the spider, tho' its web so completely resembles it. They have the spider however, & I saw a species of Tarantula it is one of the most venomous of the kind. Thank you for your letter dearest Adeline which I read at Candy a few days ago. I shall find another from you when I reach Calcutta.

Whether because Hampstead suited her, or because she was now firmly settled with her children, or simply because time had passed, by the summer of 1853 Mia was able to lead a normal life and treat her long disablement as a thing of the past. 'Mrs Jackson is a tall, striking person who has been a great invalid and lives in complete retirement, near Mr Vaughan, at Hampstead,' wrote Mrs Twistleton,[2] the young American wife of one of the Vaughan friends who came to know her through the Prinseps. 'She... has the greatest refinement and charm of manner, very quiet, not like Mrs Prinsep, but equally attractive in another line.' A second visit strengthened the impression. 'Perfectly delightful, very frank and loving and very fond of some persons and equally averse to others... A person who comprehends all heights and depths.' Mia was also taking trouble about her clothes. Her new American friend declared her to be 'elegant-looking without looking or dressing as if she were rich,' and an unnamed visitor reported to Dr Jackson, who reported it back to Adeline, that 'dear Mamma was looking very nice and well-dressed in a white Muslin dress and a blue Merino jacket.' The 'complete retirement' meant that she did not pay calls or go to parties. She certainly received visits. From the Little Holland House circle Watts called, and so probably did her neighbour, HH Vaughan; 'there is no-one [Mrs Prinsep and Mrs Jackson] love and admire more than Mr Vaughan,' Mrs Twistleton wrote. A steady trickle of friends and acquaintances from India also arrived, to bring or take back news and presents.

There was no letter to Adeline in June, and only brief notes in July and August, both complaining of lack of time. But in September there was some real news to convey, and a new method of conveying it. For the first time Dr Jackson took a large sheet of paper, folded it, sealed it and posted it direct to Adeline at 9 Well Walk. Hitherto her letters had always come enclosed in some other packet. Now, thanks to steamships and Lord Dalhousie's reorganisation of the Indian postal services, she was able to have an Indian letter of her own come through the Hampstead letterbox.

> Calcutta. Sept 5th 1853
> …We have not had much Rain this year in Calcutta, but in parts of Bengal where your Aunt Sophy has been residing, the rains have been very heavy, and as she suffers very much from the damp, she could not have had a more unfortunate situation, latterly she has become unwell from Face Ache and Tic Doloreux & was obliged to leave the place, & she is now living with me, & will remain here some months,[3] perhaps until January or February, by which time I hope they may be able to get some other Station. She came from her House in a Boat and had to travel 10 days through the large Rivers which are not very far from the Sea, and some of them during the Rains are 5 and seven miles across. If you look at a Map of Bengal you will observe that the whole of the lower part of it between Calcutta to Chittagong is intersected by these many streams which form the Soonderbund. Your Aunt had to pass through this part on her way to Calcutta, & she tells me that in going across one of the Rivers she was very much afraid that the Boat would be upset. The Boatmen or as they are called Dandies (not quite resembling the young gentlemen you meet in Oxford Street!) became alarmed & gave themselves up to Prayer calling out 'Allah Allah.' Your Aunt tells me that she desired them to take the Oars and to pull, & to keep firmly hold of the Sail, and with the aid of a good Servant to keep the people at their part they were carried safely across. But she did not get over her alarm until she reached Calcutta, and was able to sleep at night. Eugenie was with her & made great lamentations about never seeing her Patric again. She arrived looking very well, and

76

unchanged. Your Aunt Sophy looks thin and poorly and is a good deal changed from what she was when she landed in Feby. I am very glad to hear that you were pleased with the little notes I sent you about Ceylon. It is certainly a most beautiful Island and I was quite refreshed by my visit. I am very sorry to say that the little things which I had purposed sending you & your sisters have been returned to me from Board a ship in consequence of their having broken one of the Bottles of Preserves. I hope I shall have some other opportunity this month. Your Aunt Ellerton begged me send her kind love and thanks to all of you for your affectionate remembrance of her. She is very fond of little Julia and is delighted with the beautiful boldness of her handwriting and it certainly is very good. I like to hear that you are getting on with your music and singing; all these accomplishments if kept within bounds and not thought too much of, or used for display are all great sources of happiness and make the mind very independent of the world around. In fact that is the case with all mental cultivation.

*   *   *

Calcutta. October 4 1853

The few days that pass between the arrival of our Mail which brings the letters and the departure of the one which takes them away, are so fully occupied that I have scarcely time to finish what I have to do, and am obliged to write my letters at any hurried moment that I can find. I must try however to write today and tell you of the pleasure which your letters by the last mail afforded both to myself and your Aunt Sophie, and how very much obliged she felt for the lengthened details which you sent her about her Children - today she received the Daguerreotypes and is overjoyed - your dear Mamma can tell you what a pleasure it is to receive a Box from England, & when I paid your Aunt Sophie a visit today, upstairs, she had just received her Box - she cleared out all her little treasures and shewed me one pretty thing after another that had been sent to her. She seemed more pleased with the daguerreotypes of Hewy than of his sister, for the lower part of little Virginia's face seems to have had a twist which has somewhat altered the expression. I liked them both very much, and could but compare the admirable Crayon head of Mr Watts with the Daguerreotypes and was struck by the perfect likeness which he had produced.

By the time this reaches you dearest Adeline your Birthday will have taken place when you will be 16 quite a young lady. It gives me always such infinite gratification to receive the delightful accounts which I have from all parties about you, and to find that you are so perfect in all your willing [word omitted] to your darling Mamma. It is one of my greatest happinesses now that I am away to know that she is with you, to be such a Pattern for you all to look up to, & to cherish. I often long to make one of your number but from being disappointed last year I am afraid to make further plans. For a Birthday Present I should wish your darling Mamma to give you in both our names, a Bible of the largest size with a Crudens Concordance attached to it and Marginal Notes with parallel passages which you may alway keep and have for your own private retirement, or by your dressing table. This you must accept with the fond love of your darling Papa & Mamma

*   *   *

Calcutta. Nov 4 1853

I have received your letter, and the Book Marker which you sent me by Barry and have at once put it to its use in reading the Auto Biography of Haydon[4] which your dear Mamma sent me & which I have entered upon in my carriage drive today. It is very clearly and nicely written, and seems to have been written with the express purpose of publication, which destroys somewhat of its truthfulness. A very clever, but wayward person, with great love for his art, and genius, but by neglecting the common rules of prudence he falls into every kind of difficulty, and disgrace, and at last into habits, which destroy his success and lead to the destruction of his own life, whilst he attributes his reverses and trials to the opposition of his Rivals, as far as I have read. There is however much to interest, and the anecdotes which I have seen extracted from the Book, in some of the Journals, are admirably detailed. The struggles of young Artists are for the most part like those of Poets, and the higher order of painting quite ranks in the same field with that of poetry, both the offspring of cultivated minds, with high imaginative powers. The Study of a beautiful Historical picture always affords great pleasure and is I think more difficult to produce than the beautiful imagery of the Poet, for there is the Artist's touch needed; as well as the life of Haydon shews how difficult and laborious it was to attain the former - the earlier studies of his dry Bones - or Plaister of Paris figures, and the Anatomical plates shew that there is no Royal road even for Genius to acquire perfection & that every one who wishes for success must labour hard & this of itself induces talent. The knowledge of this is a vast encouragement to the diligent. This is the time of year that I always forward some little Money token of my Love, for you and your dear Sisters to spend the way you like best, making a present to you of a Gown or anything else you think most suitable. I have this year added 5 £ to your especial purse to enable you to buy some good standard works which you wish to have... I hope you will all have a merrymaking and drink Papa's health on Christmas day, and I shall think of all the dear ones at No. 9 Well Walk on that day.

References

1. Mia's father had played a part in making American ice available to Calcutta; he was a member of the Committee set up in the early 1840s to establish an Ice House, for which members of the public eagerly subscribed. The ice came as ballast in huge blocks from the Wenham lakes, inland from Boston.

2. E. Twistleton. *Letters Written to Family*. London, 1928, p.105. Following quotations, p.119 and 121.

3. Sophie was pregnant.

4. Benjamin Haydon, 1786-1846, historical painter, left a vast and colourful journal subsequently edited by Tom Taylor and published in 1853. It was avidly read in London literary and artistic circles. Mia may have thought that Haydon's description of his anatomical studies would interest her husband. (Dr. Jackson passed the book on to Mrs. Ellerton, who finished it, without comment, at the beginning of February.)

The Flying Dak (The mail by relay of men and horses).

(v) January to June 1854[1]

Calcutta also had its Christmas festivities. Between Christmas and New Year 1854 Dr Jackson gave two dinner parties, and early in January he took his aunt to dine with the Charles Prinseps - thirty-two at dinner - though they left 'very quietly' before the dancing began afterwards.[2] A couple of days later Mrs Ellerton's maid was married, Dr Jackson giving her not only a 'very handsome' present of money, but also 'the canary bird that she took so much care of for him.' Sophie Dalrymple meanwhile was awaiting the birth of her baby and her husband, returned from East Bengal, was again living in the house.

Calcutta 4th Jan 1854

Our Christmas here has now passed a very different one to yours in England where very probably you have had frost & snow upon the Ground. Whilst in my House I have not had the fire lighted. It has however been very cool and pleasant & the Ladies & Gentlemen take their walk across the Park or Plain in front of Calcutta, which in reality is as cheerful a place as can be found in a hot country. There is every variety of Carriage, and every style of dress, from the rich turbanned natives clad in the most beautiful Dacca Muslin, to the dirty black Coolie without almost a vestige of Clothes upon him. I take my ride every morning which consists of a Gallop round the plain; after which I get into my Carriage and enter upon the day's duties. I meet your Aunt Sophie at Luncheon and again at Dinner & this is about all that I see of her. She is very well and has improved very much since the cool weather set in. She has been busy in getting some Nightdresses made for you & I hope by this time next month to be able to despatch them. In your Mamma's Letter I have enclosed the cost of the Trimming which I thought she would like to see... I often long to be with you & would not stay in this country long, if I felt that I could get away, but as I have no purpose now of returning again to India when I once leave it, I shall have to stay on a little while yet, & in the mean while you have my anxious thoughts and tender wishes. I want your dear Mamma to send me a Stereoscope of herself... I have the pencil sketch of your Mamma which is very beautiful and like all Mr. Watts's productions is perfect as a work of Art but I should now like to have a sketch, Nature

Charles Prinsep

and the Stereoscope will give me the best idea which I can form. I have the daguerreotypes of yourself and your sisters & if you have no Copies of them at home you will be amused when I bring them home to see how you have grown out of your former self.

Two days after this letter was written, the Dalrymple baby was born. Mrs Ellerton was disturbed at prayer by a loud knocking at her door, and there was John Dalrymple, inviting her to go up and see his wife and new born son. 'They never before asked me to see either of their former Babes and are growing kinder in their manner toward me,' she noted hopefully. The happy flurry of the next few days, with Sophie's friends in and out of the house, was interrupted by one of Mrs Ellerton's attacks of spasms, requiring an hour's conversation with 'dear John' as soon as he came back from his rounds (though by then she was feeling better) and by the news from England that Adeline had mumps. This produced a quick note of sympathy from her father, with the information that he was sending her 'half a dozen Night Gowns which I think you will find very becoming.'

The halcyon period of the Dalrymple baby's birth did not last long. It was no time before Mrs Ellerton was fuming about John Dalrymple's manners, and indeed his morals, and the fuming went on for as long as the Dalrymples were in the house. He left the breakfast table as soon as he had finished eating, without a word to her or anyone else, he dined out without his wife ('my husband preferred to stay at home, unless I was with him'), his opinions were worse than Mohammedans or Hindus, he tried 'acting like another Pattle' to seduce his wife's maid (the last surely an implausible story if the maid was still the fat Eugenie) and he was not straightforward. There was also a minor drama of a different sort over a Ball given by Mrs Peacock, the wife of the Legal Member of the Governor's Council. The Peacocks pressed Mrs Ellerton to come, if only for an hour, but she felt obliged to refuse, 'for though no-one would have asked me to dance, yet my presence would have sanctioned it,' and waltzes and polkas were immodest; there was 'too much closeness between Man and Woman.' It was some consolation - for she liked both the Peacocks, and the temptation to accept was real - to wake up the next morning feeling particularly well, while Sophie Dalrymple, who had gone, was fit for nothing but 'lounge and languish' and did not appear until dinnertime.

Still, there were occasional outings of a different kind. On one February evening Dr Jackson had ordered dinner early so that he might take his aunt to the Town Hall to hear a lady read passages from Macbeth and sing songs and ballads, and the performer (modestly dressed in black velvet) had pleased them both. But such jaunts were rare. There was a good deal of social life of a sort: a doctor might call and 'stay tiffin' (on one occasion the visitor was carried off by Dr Jackson to see 'some great Natives and their houses and Tanks where they have tame fish who eat out of your hand') and there were usually friends or connections of friends living in the house, but it was all fitted into the interstices of work. After a dinner party in March, Mrs Ellerton noted that 'we had more conversation than we have had for months past.'

The Dalrymples moved out at about this time, with some improvement in relations, for a small dinner party that they gave afterwards was declared very pleasant. But April and May were not upon the whole good months. Dr Jackson had a day of fever, Mrs Ellerton had fainting fits, and the maid who had married at the beginning of the year died, attendance at her deathbed preventing Mrs Ellerton from going to the Dalrymple christening, though Dr Jackson managed both. His patients too seem to have been unusually demanding. On Easter Sunday he received a summons from Sir Laurence Peel, the Chief Justice, who lived the best part of an hour's carriage drive away; he escorted his aunt to church, saw her home and fitted in another patient before answering it. On another occasion, when Mrs Ellerton had been dining out herself, she returned to find him sitting down to his own dinner at 10:30. His family correspondence suffered in consequence.

Calcutta April 4 1854

The last Mail went away without any letter from me, & this may occasionally happen for I am not quite my own Master of my time and very frequently when I purpose doing one thing I am called off to perform another. It is however never willingly that I allow your Mail to go without its little letter to you and to your sisters. I am always glad to receive your packets and the present Mail I am glad to say speaks of your being well again, & I am glad to see you are so busily employed in your Drawing and Music for I know that other things also have their proper attention. The drawing from the Model will remind you of Haydon & the difficulties which he encountered & the success which afterwards followed his labours. Under such good Guidance as Mr. Watts added to your other teachers I have no doubt you will succeed altho' your first attempts may not be altogether as you could wish. Perseverance induces Talent of itself alone, & no Excellence was ever attained without the former... By the Mail I sent you some little Nightdresses and some Silk Handkerchiefs for dear Mamma which I hope have reached you safely. I have some dresses ready & they will be forwarded as soon as I can obtain from your Aunt Sophy some handkerchiefs which I am having prepared for you & Mamma. I was at your Aunt's this morning, & found her very well, she had been to a little party last night & was complaining a little of fatigue but she was looking very well, and is very happy with her Baby, who is a very pretty Child like little Virginia. You seem to have had a great many visitors from India and now & then they write to tell me that they have been to Hampstead, and they all speak of the pretty place that you have got to live in. . . I have omitted to mention in one of my letters that one of the most convenient hanging maps for you to have in the School room is called the Large Commercial Map. It is after the principle of Mercator clearly shewing both the new & old world at the same time but being of a large size. The Countries and places are more clearly delineated. Will you tell dear Mamma also to get for you if you require it in the School Room a pair of Good Globes from Richardsons for 6 or 8 guineas: I intended to have mentioned this before. Whilst war seems likely to be carried out between Russia & the other powers a knowledge of the Geographical position will add very much to your Interest.[3]

*   *   *

Calcutta May 29 1854
I was unable to write to you by this last Mail, and it often happens that I have scarcely a moment for any other than my daily duties to attend

to. The only time which I have for writing being between 3 & 4 o'clock in the Afternoon, & very frequently I am too tired to employ it in this way. By the present Mail I am sending a Box to England and I have sent as a present to you a very spirited painting of a Seek [Sikh] Horseman which was painted by a Lady in Calcutta, whom we know very well, & who I think is known to your Aunt Louisa - Mrs Turnbull. She is greatly skilled in the art of painting Horses, & has amongst her pets a number of large Squirrels who are very obedient to her orders, and are as docile as any Dog, knowing their own names, coming to her when called, & performing a variety of little Tricks which they have been taught. The Picture that I have sent you I hope will arrive safely, and ornament your little room. I daresay when Mr. Watts next calls you will be disposed to shew it to him tho' the Style is very different. It is not I think devoid of much talent.

After a month of very pleasant weather we have been afflicted during the last few days with extreme heat, and this has quite prostrated me, so that I think of last May I spent in Ceylon, and long greatly to pass no more in India - & with God's blessings I hope I shall not for I shall try very hard to get home next year.

The morning after this letter was written, Dr Jackson had to deal with an emotional scene before breakfast. It was his aunt's eighty-second birthday, and had started calmly enough with the arrival of flowers and a 'sweet little note' from the girls of the Asylum, for whom she ordered a holiday. There followed a large packet that proved to contain a request from the Ladies of the Asylum's Committee of Management that she would allow her portrait to be painted, and this request was supported by the signatures of the Governor General himself, Lord Dalhousie, all the members of his Council, the Judges and all the 'Principal Ladies and Gentlemen of Calcutta.' She had been warned a few days before by Mrs Peacock that some such request was in the air, but had not expected anything of this grandeur and she was overwhelmed. She burst into tears and 'went to prayer. When just alone, dear John came in about 8 o'clock to congratulate me with a kind salute and seemed surprised at my weeping and sobbing and seemed almost ready to weep himself - but he begged me to be calm and not allow myself to be excited. I said I had not made any sacrifice I had not undergone any self denial to have

85

such an honour conferred on me... I tried to be calm but feared it was a temptation of Satan.' Fortunately she had collected herself by the time of the birthday dinner party that evening, and in the event the sittings for the portrait - there were eighteen of them - kept her happy and interested for the next couple of months. This was just as well, for in June her beloved nephew was unexpectedly offered the opportunity of visiting the Upper Provinces without expense to himself (though it is not clear how this was arranged) and would be out of reach for six weeks.

References

1. After a nine year break Mrs. Ellerton's diary resumes at the end of 1853, so that from then onwards we know a good deal more about life at 14 Chowringhee Road.
2. Charles Prinsep, Thoby's younger brother, was Advocate-General.
3. This is the only reference in the letters to what was to become the Crimean war. England had entered the war in March, but the news had not yet reached India. On 25th March (two days before England's entry) Mrs. Ellerton noted "Dear John finished an account of Russian aggression with Turkey. They have oppressed the Christians."

Dak Bungalow (A rest house for travellers)

86

(vi) July 1854

After an early breakfast with his aunt, Dr Jackson set off on his travels on July 6th. Ten days later he sat down to write to Adeline from Meerut, more than halfway across India. He covered fifteen sides of large paper, folded and sealed them, and despatched them to Hampstead. Since the seal was cut off on arrival and the surrounding paper torn, a few sentences at the end of this vast and varied travelogue remain fragmentary.

Meerut July 16 1854

It is long since I have been able to write to you, but your dear Mamma will have told you how fully occupied I have been, and even my last letter to her was scarcely more than a few words to say that I was on my Journey, and that I was keeping well.

Journeying in India is so different from anything you have known in England that I daresay a little sketch of my travel this far would interest you. On the 6th of July I left Calcutta, and crossed over the River Hoogly to Hourah which is opposite Calcutta & where many years ago I was Resident, the Railway was to be opened that morning. The Manager Mr. Stephenson who went home with you from India, having said he would order the Railway to start either on the 6th or 7th as might suit me it suited me to start on the 6th and as I was told it would leave at 7 o'clock I was in readiness to be off at the Appointed time. There was however some delay, they had not taken in water sufficient & the Railway Carriage in second Class was not quite ready and we had to wait until 1/4 to 8 o'clock. There was an immense concourse of all classes who had never seen a Railway before, and amongst them was myself. I daresay your dear Mamma if she had been there would not have liked my going on the first time of trial on the Indian Railroad with a Carriage. There were several that did seem rather alarmed; but as there were 2 Members of Govt. Col Low & Mr and Mrs Grant[1] and all the Principal Engineers of the Railway depart[t] besides several of the Wives of the Railway Officers, & two English Steersmen it seemed as if we had secured everything against accident, and we must leave the rest to Providence.

We started at 1/4 to 8 & went on very pleasantly and slowly for some time and stopped for 5 minutes at the old Danish Station of Serampur (a place remarkable for having given shelter to the 3 first Baptist Missionaries Mr. Carey, Marshman and Ward who came out to India and were not allowed to remain in the Company's territories). In Serampur we took in some of the Railroad Contractors and we then passed on to the French Settlement of Chandernagore where all the Beauty & Fashion of the Station was assembled at the station to greet us. After a short time we passed by another Station, but with so much quickness that we scarcely saw who were waiting. We soon got to the end of our Journey which was a distance of 38 miles & this we accomplished in an hour & 20 minutes very pleasantly and safely. We had a cheerful party on Board, and about 32 Passengers in the one Carriage which as I said was a second Class one very cool, & well ventilated and about 9 feet high. Altho' the day was hot yet the motion created a breeze and made me feel cool & I thought how cold the Railway carriage travelling must be in England.

At the end of the Railway Journey my real travels and fatigues were to begin - first of all I had to walk a quarter of a mile to meet a Gig which had been sent to meet me, then I had to drive 7 miles to the Bungalow of one of the Railroad Contractors & there I met his Wife who had not been long in the Country waiting for her Husband's return, & I staid & had luncheon off a Beefsteak, made from a Fowl and Veal Cutlets made from another Fowl in the Country where there is nothing but Poultry every imaginable dish is made from a Fowl. I rested myself here for one Hour- and then got into a Palanquin carried by 4 men being 3 Changes of them who had to carry me 22 miles at the rate of 4 miles an hour - in the course between 5 & 6 hours I got to the end of this part of my Journey and reached the place whither I had the day previous sent my Travelling Carriage containing Bed etc. accompan[d] by my head table Servant Ningam who your Aunt Sarah & dear Mamma recollect who was delighted to accompany me in my tour to the Upper Provinces. I reached the Station at 10 o'clock & immediately had my carriage drawn out, & made myself comfortable for the night by putting on a dressing Gown & lying down in the Bed. These carriages are commonly used now for travelling up the Country instead of the Old System of Palanqueens, & there are 2 Companies, who have always a set of Horses along the road at distances of six miles to carry on the Conveyance. They are not Expensive much cheaper and more Expeditious than the old plan. I engaged my Carriage in Calcutta from the North Western Company, for 300Rs, or £30 to take me from Calcutta to Agra a distance of 800 miles.

After leaving Burdwan at the Commencement of my Journey in my Travelling carriage I found the road very bad - there had been a heavy fall of rain - & it was like so much deep sand or Mud. I often thought I should have to remain all night. The Coachman was a Mild tempered man, & did not use the Whip, & the Syce who accompanied the Horse first patted the Animal, then spoke to him in the most coaxing manner calling him his Brother, Sister etc. told the Horse he had not far to go, to try this once to excel himself, and by dint of help at the wheels and coaxing the Horse we at last got through our difficulty and reached the end of our six mile stage. The next stop was equally hard, & the syce not so ready with his tongue but a harsh man & he beat the poor Animal & so we stuck fast and must have remained if we had not got the help of some people by the road to raise the Carriage out of the swamp and help us on. Every day brought fresh instances of the different Kinds of management made use of in getting the Horses along and I invariably remarked that it was the same as in Human life, & that Persuasion Firmness and Kindness always did most in effecting its end. Tho to be sure there was one or two instances where a good whipping was a very effective stimulus.

I journeyed on in this way for 4 nights & four days sometimes making a very good run & once or twice taking 21/2 hours to get over 6 miles. The weather was particularly cool & pleasant, the Sky was cloudy & the roads for the most part in Excellent order except where they were undergoing repairs which was very frequently met with, as this is the season for repairing the roads. In all such cases where the road was bad I had no difficulty in getting the aid of Coolies to draw on the Carriage and as I paid them well, I got over the difficulties very soon. My friends in Calcutta all exclaimed against my Journey in such a bad time of the year one said that I should never reach Benares another that I should be detained for a day or more waiting for the falling of the Mountain Torrents, whilst a third said that the Heat would be dreadful & that I was sure to get Fever. I expected that I might meet with some difficulties but that if the Horses did not fail me, that I should make out the Journey very well and as we had rain every day in a deluge during the Month of June and the weather had been clear for 5 days, the probability was that I sh^d have fine weather all the way & so it proved & I could not have had a more enjoyable Trip, and instead of being 8 days for the first 400 miles I was only 4 days.

I reached Benares on the 4th day, and there I remained with an old friend of mine Dr Leckie who entertained me most hospitably after 4 days & 4 nights travelling, it was a relief certainly to have all the comforts of a Home and an easy Couch to lie upon for in my Journey I only waited for 2 hours every morning to take Breakfast and then went on again being satisfied with a Biscuit & Glass of Water for the rest of the day. Every 14 Miles along the road there is a Travellers Bungalow or cottage which is always conveniently situated as regards the road, and everything is very comfortable. There is a Book in which each Traveller writes down his name & the Sum he is charged with which is about one Shilling for the use of the House to take Breakfast, besides one shilling more to the Servant for the Hot Water Toast & Milk - for I always carried my own Tea & Sugar - & then for the Man who supplied the Water etc Six Pence was given all very reasonable, & comfortable.

After reaching Benares I visited the New College, & saw there the bust of James Prinsep[2] which your Aunt Julia gave me & which I gave to Charles Prinsep for the Benares College. Then I went to visit another Institution of the Educational Kind where the Scriptures are read founded by Mr. Corrie, & I promised the Principal to send him a Picture or Lithograph of Mr. Corrie on my return to Calcutta. At the Govt. School or College the Scriptures are not read lest it might be supposed the Govt. were desirous of interfering with the religion of the People. In one part of the Missionary Institution I found a number of Hindoo Girls reading the Bible in the Hindustani language, sensible nice looking children and very intelligent. The Hindoos and Mussulmen for the most part in India never allow their Girls to be taught either to read or write but desire they should [be] brought up in dark ignorance. Some of them are naturally very clever, and have a famous use of their tongue, for however ignorant they may be as to Letters and grammar they are great scolds & sometimes very quarrelsome, but the Wives of the richest & highest Hindoo like the wife of the lowest consider it no degradation to sit down & slice the Cucumber, Cut up the Potatoes & other vegetables for dinner Holding a peculiar kind of Curved Knife between their Toes. Ignorant always as they are and may be they have great Influence on their Husbands, and not less than the Wives of England.

Whilst at Benares I called upon the Rajah and another Native of Rank, & the next morning they sent me several trays containing one Tray Almonds & Raisins, in another Cashew nuts, in a third a large quantity of crystallized sugar, beautiful Lychees in a fourth & fruit in a sixth with an Intimation that they proposed calling upon me in the Course of the day. This they did, & after a short interview when they spoke of the wonders of the Electric Telegraph & Railway etc. they departed shaking hands. As soon as I reached Benares I sent down a Message by the Electric Telegraph to Mr. Halliday the Governor of Bengal to announce my arrival. This is something new since dearest Mamma left India. It extends up to Delhi. After leaving Benares I got into my travelling Carriage & as the Horses were very good & the roads smooth I made great Progress & got early the next morning to Allahabad. Here I had to cross the Ganges again having crossed it first at Benares. The Ganges & Jumna join here & Allahabad lies in the corner between them. It is a very pretty neat Station and reminds me of an English village in parts. The next place of Importance I came to was Cawnpore-once a very large Military Station. Here there was a very heavy fall of Rain and I rested for the day and spent it very pleasantly with a Friend of mine Dr Angus who entertained me most hospitably.

I determined to lose no time after quitting Cawnpore and hurried on the driver, so that I frequently went 7 or 9 miles an hour and I hoped to reach Agra the following morning. Whilst about 80 miles from Agra I was met by a special Messenger requesting me to go to Meerut instead of Agra and see the Sick Son of a Rich Banker, so here was an alteration of plans and I had a Journey of 180 miles instead of 80. I found that there was an Express of Horses along the road as the poor man's son was sick unto death. I soon got over the Journey and I reached Meerut where I am now, yesterday at noon. I came to the Hotel and there sent to the Banker to say that I had arrived. His Expression was that I was like the Rising Sun to a man in the depth of darkness, & that Words failed him to express his gratitude for the trouble I had undergone in coming to see his son. Natives in India however great their wealth, never shew any signs of its existence in their daily habits or dress. This Rich Man was but meanly clad in a somewhat dirty Muslin. He had a

91

large Emerald ring on his finger and a string of beads round his neck these likely on account of some particular Charm attached to them than on account of their value. He was a Man in every respect of Massive build- large capacious forehead, great Intelligence combined with firmness and good temper in its Composition- a frank & pleasing Man [paper torn] and clever man, who had a sick son who had been ill six Months and who had trusted the life of this son who was so dear to him. First to the Incantations & Charms of the Priests, then to the Prostration before the Idols - to the treatment of Hindustani and Mussulman Quacks Consulting the Physicians of the great Mogul of Delhi and when these had failed then writing me to come up from Calcutta, as the only European Medical Officer he had confidence in, beseeching me that I would do all I could for him & when shewn the patient I found him lying on a scarlet velvet couch [paper torn] a skeleton and in the last.... & for whom Medicine... nothing more than temporary... the danger was so imminent... might not last many days... I found him a little better... made him more hopeful. The women of the Family were in a little Enclosure concealed from the public eye by means of screens and I saw how... Their influence no doubt had been the cause of nothing having been done for him for they are more Superstitious than the Men. This will I am afraid give you a little to read. I must write to darling Mamma now & not forget dear little Mary & Julia

What Dr Jackson's original plan had been when he left Meerut, what he did at Delhi and how long he spent at Agra admiring the Taj Mahal remain unrecorded. When he next wrote to Adeline he was on his way back to Calcutta.

Ghazipore Augt 10 1854

I received your long letter giving me an account of your visit with your Aunt Virginia, yesterday at Benares which by water is about 75 miles from Ghazipore, the place where you were born and where we lived for several years, and after having once left it, I little thought I shd. ever see it again. On my way down the River Ganges, we came to it last Evening, and I got up early this morning that I might walk round the old station and take a Peep at our old House where you were born, and where you were so ill that for many many days neither your darling

Mamma or myself thought you would live to grow to be the Comfort and Happiness you have been and God Grant may always be to us both. The House is close upon the River and was looking prettier than any other place that I visited, so that I was quite pleased at finding our old Home looking so clean and nice. This is the place famous for Rose Water, and I bought some and shall send home a Batch especially for your own use, as a memento of the place where you were born, which is famous all over India & now in England for the perfume of its Rose water. I am now finishing my pleasant Journey some account of my first part I wrote to you from Meerut; and I have sent your dear Mamma some notes on the remainder. My breather has been very favourable and altho' I had not much to complain of from the fatigue in dak travelling yet it is very pleasant to feel the care and comfort of the Steamer, for I have a very nice Cabin and the Weather is very cool. I should have preferred a voyage through a part of the Country that I had never seen before, for this is not a very interesting route and I have run it several times before. The River is very broad; in some places four & five miles between the Banks and the Current very strong which is v. fortunate as one of our Engines is broken and we have only one which I think will delay therefore our journey to Calcutta and make us perhaps a day and a half longer than we otherwise should have been. I enclose you a little sketch of the Taj which I brought with me from Agra...

At 6 am on August 16th Dr Jackson called on the friends with whom his aunt had been staying during his absence to announce his safe return. Mrs Ellerton was not at her best. She had been aggrieved a couple of days before to discover that he had told Sophie Dalrymple and not herself when he might be expected, and she was not at all well. He was immediately called upon to examine her throat (which he 'rubbed plentifully with caustic') and he was back again at midday. Even after she was moved home she remained in a rather fragile state, keeping her numerous visitors at bay and dining off bread sopped in claret and water, but before the week was out life had returned to normal and she could write 'Dined with dear John alone and felt very happy.'

References

1. Colonel John Low, of the Madras Army, was a member of the Governor-General's Council. J.P. Grant was Secretary to the Government in the Home Department.
2. James Prinsep, 1799-1840, another of Thoby's brothers, worked in the Calcutta Mint, of which he became Assay Master. He was a notable orientalist, working on the ancient alphabets of India and editing the Journal of the Asiatic Society of Bengal; also something of an architect/engineer, responsible (at least in part) for bridges, a canal and the reconstruction of ancient monuments. Prinsep's Ghat (or Wharf) was named in his honour.

River steamer, the Mirzapore

(vii) September 1854 - April 1855

Pleased as she was to be home, Mrs Ellerton had much enjoyed her time away. Colonel Forbes, her host, had been in charge of the Calcutta Mint for many years and was an old friend, and she was particularly fond of his wife, a member of the Asylum's Committee of Management and an ally in various other good works. The Bishop had taken her to visit the Normal School, where she had seen four of her girls from the Asylum in class, she had driven out with Mrs Peacock, and had several games of chess with the civil surgeon who kept an eye on the Asylum, and, as she discovered, had had the original idea of the portrait ('he is a kind and benevolent man but I do not like his eccentricities, nor the house on the opposite side of the road to his for I fear there is a Hindoo lady in it'). She had had the final sittings for the portrait, and had taken the painter all over the Asylum to decide where it should hang; she enjoyed surprising him, when he asked 'whether any Gentlemen had the management of so large an institution,' with the information that 'Ladies managed the whole.' But all this paled in comparison with an invitation in Lord Dalhousie's own hand to dine at Government House. Praying for grace to bear the honour conferred upon her, she made one of a party of twenty-eight, was handed in to dinner by one of the Judges, was asked to take wine first by the Bishop and then by the Governor General himself, and afterwards invited to sit by him on the ottoman, while he and the Bishop talked about the Crimean war and she explained that while she could dine out with care she could not go to late parties. He clearly found her good value, for two more invitations to Government House followed, and he made a point of introducing his daughter to her. All this gave great satisfaction. If, as she believed, she had at one point 'lost caste,' it was now beyond question re-established.

There seem to have been fewer people than usual living "at Jackson's" during the last quarter of the year: only one lady with a child and later another who was expecting and in due course produced a baby.[1] There were thus more tête à tête evenings for aunt and nephew. They also went out together on a number of occasions - an evening party at the Lieutenant Governor's; a concert at the house of one of the Government Secretaries, with a thrilling performance of Handel's *Comfort Ye*; a visit to the collection of Indian artefacts prepared for the forthcoming Paris exhibition; a lecture on Nineveh by one of the chaplains, a man whom Dr Jackson had had to stay for three weeks in the Spring when he was in a low state after the departure of his family; and, to Mrs Ellerton most exciting of all, a trip on the new railway. Dr Jackson had arranged this ('he is a precious generous kindhearted soul') and took her, a friend, her maid and her *khitmutgar* together with his own butler, coachman and two other Indian servants for an hour's journey up the river to Hooghly. The starting whistle had been alarming, but the trip itself most agreeable, through beautiful country, the rice fields turning from green to yellow, with crowds of spectators along the line and a little sightseeing and an excellent tiffin awaiting them at the end; 'no fretting, no hurry,' and everyone back safely by 5:15, not at all tired. It was a pleasant and relatively serene period, notwithstanding a drama at the Asylum that preoccupied Mrs Ellerton for several weeks. Criticism of a newly-arrived teacher by a member of the Management Committee - unjust, Mrs Ellerton suspected - triggered a series of resignations and the crisis was only brought to an end when she volunteered to take on the Secretaryship and Treasurership herself, a skilful move that brought everyone to their senses. Dr Jackson was kept posted about all this, giving required approval at intervals, but in general remaining 'taciturn.'

Did Mrs Ellerton realize that he was planning to go home as soon as he could manage it? Probably not, or not fully. Neither aunt nor nephew went in for premature fretting. Whatever the uncertainties, nothing was to be gained by discussing them, and the uncommunicative Dr Jackson would have said as little as possible until all was settled. Everything went on as before. But the letters to Adeline show the direction of her father's mind.

Calcutta Sep^t 1854

I must write and tell you that by the present Mail I have sent you a little Signet Ring engraved with your name in Persian on one side & Old

English on the other. This I had made for you at Delhi and I now send as a keepsake which you must never part with but remember it as a Souvenir of my visit to Delhi in 1854... I was so glad to get the letter from your dear Mamma informing me that you were all on your way to the Seaside. I hope that this will do you much good & that you will have no return of pain in your head. I can fancy what a happy family you will all be, & the New Scenery of Wales will in itself be inspiriting to you. I dislike fashionable watering places of any kind and I should have no fancy ever to go and see Brighton with a view of staying at it. The Gowns would do very well for the seaside & I am glad to learn that they are so soon to be put to good use...

Your Aunt Sophy and Baby are very well, they are still in Calcutta. Your Uncle Henry Bayley is likely to be here by the end of the Month so there will be quite a gathering. Your Aunt Sophy was very much pleased with your long letter. She is not very fond of writing herself but likes very much to hear from you. I was very glad to find you had been present at the opening of Crystal Palace[2] and had enjoyed it so much. I should scarcely have thought you would have been able to wear the Puttis & Cape on such an Occasion.

*   *   *

Calcutta Oct 4 1854

I have just received your dear Mamma's letters dated August 20th informing me that you had been again laid up with sore Throat attended with a rash like the Nettle rash. I am sorry to find that this has been the case, but I sh^d fancy that plenty of walking exercises would be the best thing for you provided it fell short of fatigue... If I should be with you next year & we keep well & can afford it, I think we must all journey up to the Lakes of Cumberland, & pass a short time on our way thither at one of the Northern watering places. I have seen very little of my own Country & before I came out to India I had no Opportunities of visiting & I therefore look forward with some pleasure to the time when this Opportunity may be afforded me, increased as the [illegible] then would be in having you all as Companions of my voyage. Your dear Mamma tells me that you are all going to the Devil's Bridge not far distant... In all Mountainous countries there is a vast amount of superstition. It is very marked amongst the Scotch & I suppose the

Welsh are not without it. But of all countries there is none equal to India where it pervades every thing even the common duties of life. There was a remarkable Omen taken from the flight of Birds in the last Battle against the Seeks. A flight of Wild Geese in the most beautiful order (as I daresay you will have an opportunity of witnessing in Wales) passed over the British Army previous to Battle, without breaking line, but whilst over the Seek army, the regularity was disturbed & they became a confused mass, & it was immediately augured that the Victory would be on the side of the English. This happened at the Battle of Goojerat in the Punjab.

*   *   *

Calcutta Nov 6 1854

...My time is occupied a good deal now and I do not expect to have any new Holiday until I leave India, for I have no desire to pay any other visit to the Upper Provinces and the desire which I had, to visit China and New South Wales has subsided into the wish of coming home and passing my time with darling Mamma and all the Children. When I shall be able to accomplish this, I cannot tell, but I seem to feel that it is nearer than I at one time expected. I have just had the Photograph of yourself and find very little in the features and appearance to remind me of the little Girl whose delight it used to be to dress herself in my Coat & Waistcoat and come into the dining [room] to surprise your dear Mamma & myself... Tell Mary & Julia that I shall write to them next Mail, & that I hope they will have a very merry Christmas.

*   *   *

Calcutta Decr 5 1854

I was very much grieved last night at receiving the accounts of the sad Illness which has befallen darling Mamma; & to find that she had suffered so much & been confined to her Bed for so long. It must have been a very trying and anxious time for you all, & the irritability of Stomach continuing for so long a time and unrelieved by any Medicine must have alarmed you greatly... It is a very exhausting disease and some time is always required before a Person gets well and a little Change for a week or two at Brighton may have been considered necessary. I look very anxiously for every Mail, and I feel the time very long since you all left me. I have been so much and so long alone that it has seemed as if it were always to remain so. I do hope however that this year will be my last in India and that next summer I may have the happiness of spending the time with you all and going with you to some pleasant and cheerful place for the hotter months. Next month I shall be able to decide and we will say nothing more about it now... I shall be unable to write to dear Mary or Julia - give them a kiss from me and my love to you for all your tender care to darling Mamma during her Illness.

The Calcutta Christmas was rather quieter this year than the year before. Mrs Ellerton had three little girls from the Asylum to stay for their holidays; she took them out shopping to spend the money that Dr Jackson had given them and played word games with them in the evening when he dined out. As before, aunt and nephew dined with the Charles Prinseps in the new year, but more quietly since Mrs Prinsep was on the point of having a baby, and later in the week they went to another small dinner party with Sir Lawrence Peel's successor as Chief Justice, Sir James Colvile, at which 'the Tagores' were among the few guests, the only Indians to appear on the social scene recorded in Mrs Ellerton's diaries. This was probably Prosunna Coomar Tagore, a lawyer and philanthropist much in evidence in Calcutta public life, but possibly Devendranath (father of the poet Rabindranath) who had raised the funds to send the first Medical College students to England, and had not yet set out on his Himalayan travels in pursuit of spiritual enlightenment. Mrs Ellerton makes no comment, but it was almost unheard of for a Hindu to break caste rules and eat with the English at this period. In between they gave an evening party themselves, and Mrs Ellerton lunched at Government House. But then, a fortnight or so later, Dr Jackson broke the news to his aunt. 'The day, the terrible day has come! that I have notice I am to part with my beloved John!' she wrote. 'After breakfast he requested to speak to me alone, and it was to tell me that he had made up his mind to join his Wife and family - that he would take me with him, or leave me at Madras. I hesitate to leave Calcutta, ...Oh! Lord be thou my guide.' The next day, after a bad night, and feeling 'not quite well,' she had to look after a stall at a Fancy Sale, but the day after that she took characteristic grip. She sent for the Bishop, by her account to tell him of her difficulties, by his, to ask him to give her quarters at the Palace. This he promptly offered. She later wished she had been rather less expeditious, for she heard bad reports of the Bishop's servants and food, and she received a warm and quite unexpected invitation from the wife of one of the Government Secretaries that she might have preferred to accept, but at least it was decided and life could go on.

Dr Jackson was too busy to write to Adeline in January. At about the time when he would normally be writing his family letters he was summoned to spend a night at Barrackpore, the Governor-General's country retreat up the river. It had been evident for some time that, for all his dynamism, Lord Dalhousie was far from well – Mrs Ellerton had picked up the rumour that he had cancer in the mouth early in September – and his own medical man now urged immediate return to Europe. Dr Jackson, called in for a second opinion, concurred. But it was an unprofitable journey, for Lord Dalhousie had no intention of taking his doctors' advice, and meanwhile work accumulated at Chowringhee Road. Apart from the whole business of winding up the practice and clearing out possessions, two patients who were also old friends were at the point of death. The Colonel Forbes with whom Mrs Ellerton had stayed the summer had a serious heart attack and Mrs Charles Prinsep died a fortnight after the birth of her baby. The February letter to Adeline was so hastily written as to be more than usually difficult to read, and indeed as he was finishing it he got it muddled up with another, signed it 'In haste, your very busy J. Jackson,' and despatched it to Henry Bayley at Dacca. But it reached Adeline in the end.

6th Feb 1855

The last mail took no letter from me to you. Indeed it sometimes happens that I have scarcely time to write to your dear Mamma... During the last few days I have been very busy getting my Books packed and trying to get some Boxes ready to go by Ship and yesterday

Daniel Wilson, Bishop of Calcutta

I went to enquire about a Cabin on Board the Steamer & tho' I find that there was not one available yet this has the appearance of a [illegible] and by the time I look to leave I daresay I shall find a place. Your aunt Sophy says I should stay on in India until the end of the year but I don't agree to this. Now if I had you all out in India I would stay for the next 3 years... Your Aunt is looking very well and the Baby beautiful the admiration & envy of all the Mammas.

Dr Jackson must have discovered his mistake soon after this letter was gone, for he wrote again, more legibly, two days later.

Calcutta Feb 8 1855

This is our pleasantest season of the year, the Sky without a Cloud, & the temperature so mild and agreeable that no Climate in the World can excel that of the Early part of February in Calcutta. It is likely [sic] the Mildest May day in England, & if there were any longer continuance we would have Calcutta visited for its delicious Climate. It passes very quickly however and before the end of the month all the Symptoms of Approaching hot weather will shew themselves. How much I should have liked for you all to have been here this Cold Weather, & we have had more than usual subjects of Interest, besides several Vocal Performances... we have had a Lady Violinist who is said to be superior to any performer that has visited India a second Paganini. Then there have been the Collection of Articles from the French Exhibition, and we have had a collection of Pictures Statues etc and works of Indian Artists arranged in the Town Hall in Humble Imitation of the Crystal palace, & lastly the Opening of the Railway. For those fond of dancing has been a series of parties. These I have not been to. Your Aunt Sophy goes to them. I have a note from her now begging me to go and see her as she had a bad cold & is afraid it will prevent her going to the Ball at Govt House. I have scarcely time to make any arrangements for Packing up my things and I have so little time to [illegible] that I must begin now in earnest. In June I hope I shall see you all.

This was to be Dr Jackson's last Indian letter to his eldest daughter. February and March were full of packing and farewell parties. Presents poured in, and were left for Henry Bayley to have packed and des-

Bishop's Palace, Chowringhee, Calcutta

103

patched.[3] There were the sort of tensions at home that might be expected when both aunt and nephew were under strain. Mrs Ellerton got into a fuss about an Ellerton nephew who was counting on help from Dr Jackson when he arrived at Calcutta. Dr Jackson was not at all pleased when a visiting teacher from the Asylum stayed too long and put out his timetable. Mrs Ellerton was upset when he refused to take a bracelet to one of her relatives in England ('He is naturally taciturn and distant and I fear has contracted a haughty manner from his wife's relations for they are all very proud') and when she suspected that he had taken Sophie Dalrymple to a concert rather than herself. But none of this was grave. There were other concerts and a row of dinner parties. In the course of March and in between the dinner parties Mrs Ellerton moved her possessions to the Bishop's Palace, and at the end of the month Dr Jackson escorted her to her new quarters, coming to pick her up for each of the five final dinner parties in the ten days running up to Easter. On Easter Sunday he joined her at church, arriving late. On Easter Monday, 'my dearest most beloved John came in about 7 o'clock and I had a cup of Tea ready for him but he could not stop to take it but took a hurried and affectionate farewell and so we meet no more in this world.'

Dr Jackson travelled by Suez and Alexandria with Colonel and Mrs Forbes under his care, the Colonel dying and Mrs Forbes almost dying on the journey. On May 23rd his ship docked at Southampton, and he was reunited with his wife and his three almost unknown daughters in a country that he had not seen for twenty-five years.

References

1. This was a Mrs. Elliott, perhaps the same about whom Dr. Jackson wrote in 1851.
2. Paxton's glass building erected in Hyde Park for the 1851 Exhibition had now been moved to Sydenham.
3. Among the presents that Henry Bayley brought to show Mrs. Ellerton after Dr. Jackson had gone was the silver inkstand, presented by some of his former students in the Medical College, that was always to stand on my father's writing table, and was later to be regularly used by Quentin Bell.

(On the central candleholder)
Presented to
Dr Jackson

(Along the pen tray)
In an humble but sincere tribute of affectionate regard
from some of the
NATIVE GRADUATES
of the
CALCUTTA MEDICAL SCHOOL
who in the practice of their profession, have so
often availed themselves of, and benefited by
his personal kindness and superior professional skill

CALCUTTA
April 1855

3
Reunion

Did they all live happily ever after? By and large, yes, as far as the human condition permits. Even Mrs Ellerton was probably not unhappy during her last years, though an attack of rheumatic fever that struck her down almost immediately after her nephew's departure left her much diminished. The domestic arrangements at the Bishop's Palace proved more comfortable than expected; the other people in the house, the Chaplain and his family, were entirely congenial, and the dear Bishop, she reported[1], was as kind as a brother. He for his part enjoyed her stories of Old Calcutta and appreciated her punctuality at meals. She liked to know that there was a south-facing room with a beautiful view in the Hampstead house that her nephew wished she were occupying, and to her friends she might throw in a reference to her "poor aching heart", but she had no doubt that she was right to stay where she was. Under the Bishop's auspices she became established in a unique position as a sort of tribal matriarch among the English of Calcutta. Almost the last entry in her diary records a visit from Lady Canning, wife of Lord Dalhousie's successor, who came to bring her news of seeing Addy Jackson in London. She lived to see the end of what she undoubtedly thought of as the Mutiny, dying in her eighty-sixth year, in 1858.

Meanwhile Dr Jackson set to work to reconstruct his life. He moved his family from Hampstead to a larger house at Hendon, tidied up his Cambridge degree so that he could now properly be styled Doctor of Medicine, established a consulting room near Hanover Square, published a small piece on the varieties of tetanus in India and was elected Fellow of the Royal College of Physicians. He may not have had many patients beyond old Indian friends, but he seems to have been regarded as the man who knew about oriental diseases and to have been accepted to some extent into the inner ring of the London medical world.[2]

106

This was not the world of Little Holland House. During the years of separation, Mia had moved - as far as she had moved at all beyond the immediate family cocoon - among people of entirely different interests and largely different values from those imprinted on her during her first years of married life. My father, living as a child under the long shadow of his great-aunts Julia Cameron and Sara Prinsep, recorded that the names of poets and artists were so often on the lips of his elders that he came to think that 'nothing was finer in the world than art or poetry.'[3] Dr Jackson did not think this. Conduct was what he minded about, and he liked facts better than speculation or ideas. None of his considerable energies were spent in questioning the rule within which he had grown up; it was evident to him that a man's treatment of parents, tradesmen, and benefactors was more important than whether he painted or wrote badly or well. Music seems to have been the only one of the arts that meant much to him. It is not necessary to be an intellectual or a cultivated or amusing man to be a good doctor, or indeed a good husband, and there is no reason to doubt that Dr Jackson was both; but it is easy to see why his youngest and ablest son-in-law Leslie Stephen judged him 'somehow a bit of an outsider.'[4] The first months after his return must have been hard going for everyone.

All the same, after all those plans for family holidays made on hot Calcutta afternoons, it is a little surprising as well as a little melancholy to find him alone in Scotland the August after his return,[5] writing to tell his dearest Addy about Liverpool and the Burns monument at Dumfries as he had once told her about the Taj Mahal; she and her sisters, and presumably Mia, were with the Prinseps in Wales. Even more remote from the Calcutta dreams was Adeline's marriage the next year to the Pattle ladies' hero, HH Vaughan. 'The most startling event of its kind since the marriage of Luther,' one of Vaughan's friends declared it,[6] for the Regius Professor was a sophisticated bachelor of forty-five with a London as well as an Oxford reputation, and the bride a quiet and pretty girl of eighteen of whom no one had ever heard. The engagement was supposed to have been engineered by Mrs Prinsep, or perhaps by her and Mia in concert (by the standards of Calcutta the age gap was nothing out of the way); but however this may be the wedding left Mia

107

Adeline Jackson, at the time of her marriage

Adeline's Parisian wedding dress

prostrated. She had leant heavily on her eldest daughter during the years when she had been on her own and Adeline had taken the weight. Dr Jackson's reply to Adeline's first letter from her wedding tour suggests that with her at least he had established an entirely easy and open relationship during the last eighteen months; perhaps also that he had taken the measure of things at home and was by now effectively if unobtrusively in charge.

28 George Street
Hanover Square
Sep 19 1856.

…I was quite sure that in a few days I should receive a Letter from you, and I had this morning that pleasure. Whilst we were anxiously looking out for the post, as this seemed the day we thought we should hear from you, and dear Mary had gone for the letters, she came running at full speed, and after crying out to her Mamma that there was a letter from you, her foot caught in her gown and she fell at the step, happily unhurt. The Letter was seized with all haste, and as it was found on being opened to be intended for myself, it was delivered into my hands, when I read the contents to dear Mamma and then gave it for the Children to look over, and amuse themselves by finding the places and learning the History of the Spots you had visited. We were all quite cheered at hearing from you, and learning from you that you were so well and so happy. No day has passed that you have not been much in our thoughts. At first dear Mamma used to wander about the house like Rachel weeping for her Child, or retire to her Room to sit down and think in Silence on the absence of her fondly loved daughter. The first week or so was very sad, but latterly she has occupied herself a good deal more, and has been busy with the Household duties or has taken to work with her needle and has come occasionally with me into Town, and she is beginning to wear something more of a cheerful Aspect. She would have derived no comfort from little Julia Cameron and it was better therefore that she should not come, as she would only have been in the way. Tender love and consideration which dear Mamma has so abundantly around her, without being teased with it, and being left to

Mary and Julia Jackson at the time of Adeline's marriage.

herself, will do her more good and has already accomplished [more] than any external or officious notice. In a little time we shall see her quite herself again. Your Aunt Louisa comes down occasionally at 10 o'clock and we are all very sorry for it - happily she has given up the practice of late.

We are all greatly cheered by your letters, and feel rejoiced at your Happiness. It must indeed be a great Enjoyment to you, to witness all these scenes of Interest, with one so able and so ready to give you all the knowledge and every explanation connected with them; and I have no doubt that the enjoyment is as fully shared by himself in having such a Companion to listen to him.

Pray give my kind regards to Vaughan and assure him of the full trust we repose in him for your welfare. We have not an anxious thought about it, but are quite sure of his tender care of you...

From this point Dr Jackson becomes all but invisible. It is Mia who is in evidence, as the friend and confidante of poets and artists, perhaps the most beautiful of the Pattle sisters as they all aged, a devoted and amusing grandmother.[7] But there are occasional glimpses of him as well. In 1861 he prescribes chlorine baths and mustard plasters for Tennyson's depression;[8] the Tennysons came from much the same Lincolnshire background as himself, and the poet had been a small boy at Louth Grammar School when he was a big one, so that among the Pattle ladies' friends they at least were not strangers. A year later Mia reports joyfully from the Camerons in the Isle of Wight that Mr Fisher has at last proposed to Mary; there was no money but he had never cared for anyone else and Mary was well fitted to be a poor man's wife. Mary later records in her diary that when her husband falls ill on their wedding tour (he had imprudently bathed in an icy Alpine stream and she had failed in her attempt to make satisfactory arrowroot), her father appears from the other side of a Swiss lake, administers quinine, reads the Sunday morning service aloud in the hotel dining room, and vanishes again to rejoin Mia and Julia, calm evidently restored. His Lincolnshire connections are clearly maintained, for when his elder brother dies in 1868 he and the younger brother are joint executors of the Will. After ten years at Hendon, the London practice is wound up and the Jacksons move to a country house, Saxonbury, at Frant, near Tunbridge Wells. Julia marries, very happily, a friend of her Fisher brother-in-law, Herbert Duckworth. Dr Jackson takes an interest in his hay and strawberries, equips a nine-year-old grandson with a chess set ('I daresay dear Mamma will shew you all the moves') and sends Adeline a substantial cheque when her husband's investments go wrong. Occasionally he escapes: to America on his own, hoping that since Mia will stay with the Patmores his absence 'will be attended with less distress than I had feared - most likely I think' and a few years later, with one of the Cameron sons, to an Oriental Congress in St Petersburg followed by a visit to Moscow and Nijni Novgorod, regretting that there is not time to return by the Volga, the Don and Constantinople as he would have liked and bringing back assorted small trophies for grandchildren. His energies remain undiminished until his eighties.

Of course there were troubles and sorrows. Mia was increasingly crippled by arthritis. Julia's husband suddenly dropped dead when she was pregnant with their third child, and she was left to a seven-year widowhood, endured with silent fortitude and dedicated attendance at the bedside of sick friends. A Vaughan son died in early childhood. Of Mary's eleven children, one became a permanent invalid whose needs ended by dominating the Fisher household. Saddest of all for her parents, Adeline Vaughan died when she was only in her forties, 'of thyroid,' in family tradition, worn out by coping with an increasingly difficult husband and their five children in a remote Pembrokeshire castle. But the good outweighed the bad. Saxonbury remained a house where the young were welcome and enjoyed staying. Julia remarried, and Leslie Stephen was taken into the family with enthusiasm. The numerous grandchildren were a lively and promising lot, most of them intelligent and some conspicuously good-looking, and their grandfather lived to see the boys well started on promising careers. The network of family affections remained as strong as such a network can be. Dr Jackson may well have felt that a taproot had been cut when his Indian service ended, but he had not made a bad job of his second life in England. Equanimity, constancy and reticence are unromantic qualities and much less attractive than the dramatic fizz and overflow-

113

Saxonbury House

ing affections of the Pattles, but they help to keep things together and make them work. For the Jacksons' descendants – Vaughans, Fishers, Duckworths, Stephens - the inheritance made an interesting and often effective mix.

At the end of 1879 Mia was seriously weakened by an attack of rheumatic fever. It soon became clear that Saxonbury must be abandoned. The Jacksons moved to Brighton, and there with Julia to nurse him and his eldest grandson, Adeline's son, at his side, Dr Jackson died in March 1887 at the age of eighty two. Mia survived him for five more years.

References

1. Letter to the Governor-General's doctor (thanking him for prodding Lord Dalhousie into subscribing to one of her charities) quoted in G. Smith, *Physician and Friend*. London, 1902, pp. 182-3
2. He was called as an expert witness in the trial of Palmer, "the Rugely poisoner" in 1856 (Stephen op cit, p. 26) and was invited by the President of the Royal College of Physicians to join a very select medical club (*B.M.J.* loc. cit.)
3. Fisher, op cit, p. 14.
4. Stephen, op cit, p. 27.
5. The excursion to Scotland was perhaps an extension of Dr. Jackson's journey to see his brothers in Lincolnshire where, according to my father, he found that his existence had been forgotten by everyone in the village. (HAL Fisher, loc. cit.). He seems to have enjoyed fitting as much into a journey as possible: in 1857 we find him going from London to join the Vaughans at Aberystwyth, via Teignmouth, Bath, Bristol and Cardiff.
6. Goldwin Smith, quoted by EGW Bill. *University Reform in the Nineteenth Century*. Oxford, 1973, Chapter 15, from which it appears that Vaughan's matrimonial intentions had been confused. At some point he had been secretly engaged to a young lady who had been reluctant to announce the engagement on the grounds that her family would disapprove. Shortly before his marriage he had been making advances to a relation of Mia's American friend, Mrs. Twistleton. The Twistletons thought he had behaved very badly and took the darkest view of the affair. (Twistleton op cit pp. 303-4). The secret fiancée and the Twistleton relation may be the same, but I think more likely not.
7. Mia's posthumous reputation seems to be for severity in youth and plaintive dependence in old age. But the Fisher grandchildren at least remembered her gaiety and affection as well as her bath-chair. "It is very dull now Granny has gone" a thirteen-year-old granddaughter wrote after one of her visits.
8. A. Thwaite. *Emily Tennyson*. London, 1996, p. 367

Dr Jackson as seen by his sister-in-law. 1864 photograph by Julia Cameron